THE COMPLETE CONTAINER GARDENING HANDBOOK

A SIMPLIFIED APPROACH FOR SMALL SPACES AND
PATIOS TO CREATE YOUR OWN URBAN OASIS OR
GROW BOUNTIFUL FRUITS AND VEGETABLES

JAKE RAGEN

CONTENTS

INTRODUCTION

In the symphony of life, our gardens often become the neglected notes, drowned out by the crescendo of daily responsibilities. As a fellow cultivator of green dreams, I understand the trials that accompany the desire to nurture nature in the midst of our fast-paced, space-constrained lives. The struggle is real, and the pain is palpable — whether it's the longing for a burst of color on a cramped balcony or the ache of watching dreams of a flourishing garden wither away in the shadows of a busy schedule.

BUCK'S SUCCESS STORY

Buck's connection with gardening was a tale of struggle, where mulching felt like a chore, transplanting a job, and watering like torture. Yet, the allure of the concrete jungle called him away to college, leaving the soil and seeds behind. But life has a way of circling back to its roots, and so it was for Buck.

Yearning to nurture nature, he ventured into the world of indoor plants, starting with a humble succulent on a windowsill. Little did he know that a small plant would be the catalyst for a newfound passion.

Moving to Knoxville, Buck found himself a poor college student in a tiny, old apartment, seemingly worlds away from the sprawling gardens he dreamt of.

Undeterred by limited space and finances, Buck discovered the magic of container gardening. Propagating plants became his mantra and was a great solution to transform his confined living quarters. With a mint cutting here and a cactus bud there, his windowsills and counters bloomed with life. Soon, what began as a modest indoor herb garden became a testament to the power of perseverance and resourcefulness.

The journey wasn't without its challenges. Buck's early forays into gardening were marked by trials, from a frost-bitten kalanchoe in a mug to throwing out a bromeliad that died but, in fact, had just begun producing pups. Yet, in those setbacks, he found invaluable lessons that would shape his understanding of the art of cultivation.

Buck's story serves as proof that container gardening is an easy, budget-friendly, and space-saving method to surround yourself with plants.

The Complete Container Gardening Handbook is your ally in transforming your gardening dreams into a vibrant, living reality. This isn't just a book; it's a bridge between the space you have and the garden you've always envisioned. Picture this: a thriving oasis of greenery adorning your windowsills, balconies, or even the tiniest corners of your living space. *The Complete Container Gardening Handbook* is your passport to this transformative journey.

Now, you might be wondering, what prompted you to pick up this book? Was it the desire to reclaim a connection with nature in the hustle and bustle of urban life? Or perhaps the realization that even the smallest space can be a canvas for a flourishing garden? Whatever the reason, the answer is sure to lie within the following pages. You'll find not only practical advice but a companion who understands your challenges and celebrates your victories.

As you leaf through these pages, envision the result: a life infused with the vibrancy of flourishing plants, a sanctuary of green amidst the concrete. The joy of harvesting your herbs, the satisfaction of watching blooms unfold, and the sense of accomplishment as you bring nature into the heart of your home —these are the rewards waiting for you.

Container gardening is a fun activity for all ages to enjoy and benefit from, whether alone for a quiet retreat or with friends and loved ones. Interacting with plants in your greenspace is a

refreshing and stimulating experience with proven health benefits for body and mind, a truly transformative activity for
everyone!

So, let's embark on this journey together. Feel the soil between
your fingers, breathe in the freshness, and know unequivocally
that this is the right book for you—the key to unlocking the
door to a greener, more fulfilling life, one container at a time.

1

THE ART OF CONTAINER GARDENING

The glory of gardening: hands in the dirt, head in the sun, heart with nature. To nurture a garden is to feed not just the body but the soul.

— ALFRED AUSTIN

WHAT IS CONTAINER GARDENING?

Container gardening, or pot gardening, is a versatile horticultural practice that involves cultivating plants, including edible ones, in containers rather than traditional ground beds. This method has become a beacon of hope for individuals facing the challenge of limited or non-existent garden space.

The primary allure of container gardening lies in its adaptability and resourcefulness. If you don't have an expansive yard or any patch of soil to call your own, this method offers a practical solution. It is space-efficient and allows you to create miniature green paradises even in the smallest living spaces. Whether in the urban jungle, suburban landscape, or within the confines of an apartment, container gardening offers you freedom and a means to cultivate a piece of nature wherever your heart desires.

Urban growers, in particular, have embraced container gardening as a creative and transformative way to infuse greenery into the concrete tapestry of city life. What makes container gardening an urban gardener's dream is its ability to transform limited spaces into thriving green sanctuaries.

The popularity of container gardening is further heightened by its accessibility to people with varying skill levels. For beginners, starting with only a few potted plants to focus on is a less intimidating entry into the world of gardening than tending to an extensive backyard. On the other hand, seasoned gardeners appreciate the flexibility of container gardening to experiment with different soil compositions, watering techniques, and plant varieties. It becomes a dynamic canvas upon which beginners and experts can practice making botanical masterpieces.

Container gardening transcends its role as a mere cultivation technique; it becomes an art form, an expression of your vision interacting with the canvas of containers. It is an affirmation that limitations need not stifle creativity in the realm of horticulture. Container gardening is a testament to the power of adaptability. It enables you to cultivate plants and a profound connection to nature in the most unexpected corners of your life.

HOW MUCH FOOD CAN YOU GROW?

The potential of home container gardening hinges on the available space's size and suitability; however, small spaces can be highly productive. Gardeners report growing upward of 184lbs of food on a six-by-eight-foot balcony and a few windowsills (Chelsea Green, 2023).

BENEFITS OF CONTAINER GARDENING

Gardening in containers has many benefits, making it a useful and fun choice for growing plants. Let's delve into these advantages, exploring how each contributes to the appeal of container gardening:

Versatility

Container gardening is incredibly versatile, accommodating many plant species and varieties. Whether you're interested in cultivating vibrant flowers, fresh herbs, or even vegetables, containers provide the flexibility to create a diverse and visually appealing garden. The ability to choose different-sized containers also adds to this versatility, allowing you to experiment with various plants to fit your space and preferences.

Mobility

One of the standout features of container gardening is its mobility. Unlike traditional gardens, where plants are rooted in the ground, containers can be moved easily. This means you can chase the sunlight throughout the day, protect delicate plants from

harsh weather conditions, or rearrange your garden's layout for aesthetic reasons. If you live in rental properties or are facing space constraints, the mobility of container gardens provides an unparalleled advantage.

Accessibility

Container gardening brings nature to your doorstep. The accessibility of container plants is a significant advantage, especially for those with limited mobility or busy schedules. The convenience of having your garden within arm's reach allows for regular, spur-of-the-moment interactions. Whether you have a balcony, porch, or a small patio, container gardening transforms these spaces into green retreats to enjoy and nurture a deeper connection with nature.

More Variety

Containers empower gardeners to experiment with a more extensive variety of plants. Different containers can cater to the specific needs of various plants, enabling the cultivation of species that might not thrive in the same garden bed. This variety extends beyond just types of plants; it includes different colors, textures, and sizes of containers, providing a canvas for creative expression and enhancing the aesthetic appeal of your garden.

Little to No Weeding

One of the most celebrated benefits of container gardening is the absence of the arduous task of weeding. Container gardens, by their nature, are less susceptible to invasive weeds that can plague traditional gardens. The controlled environment of containers minimizes the intrusion of unwanted plants, allowing you to focus more on the care and enjoyment of your chosen flora. This saves time and reduces the physical strain associated with traditional gardening chores.

Control Space Invaders

Container gardening provides a literal and figurative barrier against space invaders, namely invasive plants or pests that can infringe upon and compromise the well-being of other plants. In traditional gardens, these invasive elements can spread unchecked, leading to competition for nutrients and space and damage and crop losses. With containers, you have greater control over the growing environment, preventing unwanted pests and weeds from taking over and ensuring that each container's inhabitant thrives without interference.

Less Disease Problems

The controlled environment of container gardening contributes to a reduction in disease- related issues. Container-grown plants are less susceptible to soil-borne diseases, as the soil in containers can be easily replaced or sterilized between plantings. This starkly contrasts traditional gardens where soil-borne diseases can linger and impact the health of successive plantings. The container's isolation also limits the spread of diseases, creating a healthier and more disease-resistant growing environment.

Saves Time and Labor

Container gardening is a time-saving alternative to traditional gardening methods. The absence of extensive garden beds means less time spent on soil preparation, digging, and weeding. Additionally, the controlled environment allows for more efficient management of fertilizers and other inputs. Container gardens are well-suited for people with busy lifestyles, as they require less maintenance and can be tended to in shorter, more manageable intervals. This makes gardening accessible to a broader range of enthusiasts, including those with limited time or physical constraints.

Water Conservation

Container gardening promotes water conservation through efficient irrigation practices. Containers allow for precise control over the amount of water each plant receives,

minimizing water wastage. Unlike conventional gardens, where water may be dispersed over a larger area, container gardens direct water to the root zones, ensuring optimal hydration without excess runoff. Additionally, using water-retaining soil mixes in containers helps conserve moisture, reducing the frequency of watering and making container gardening an environmentally conscious choice.

Aesthetic Appeal

Container gardening is a visual delight, transforming any space into a vibrant and aesthetically pleasing haven. The variety of containers, from classic terracotta pots to modern, sleek designs, allows for creative expression and customization. The plants, arranged in containers of different shapes, sizes, and colors, add layers of visual interest. Even edible gardens can be a feast for the eyes. Whether cultivating a symmetrical arrangement on a balcony or a diverse mix of containers in a courtyard, the aesthetic appeal of container gardening contributes to the overall beauty of your living environment.

Improved Soil Quality

Container gardening provides the opportunity to optimize and control soil quality, a critical factor in plant health. Unlike traditional gardens, where soil conditions may vary, containers allow you to tailor the soil mix to suit the specific needs of each plant. This control over soil quality promotes better nutrient absorption, root development, and overall plant growth. It also mitigates the challenges associated with poor or depleted soil, ensuring your plants thrive in an environment conducive to their well-being.

Indoor Gardens

Container gardening transcends the boundaries of outdoor spaces, offering the possibility of creating lush indoor gardens. From windowsills to countertops, indoor container gardens bring the beauty of nature into your living spaces. This adds a touch of greenery to indoor environments and contributes to improved air quality. Indoor container gardens are precious for people with limited outdoor space or those residing

in climates where outdoor gardening may be challenging for a significant portion of the year.

Design Accents

Containers are versatile design elements, allowing you to introduce unique accents and focal points in your overall landscape or home decor. The choice of containers, whether eclectic or coordinated, can complement the architectural style of your home or the theme of your garden. Containers can be strategically placed to define pathways, create boundaries, or accentuate specific features. Moreover, they offer a dynamic canvas for seasonal changes, enabling you to refresh your space with new plant selections or decorative elements, enhancing the visual appeal with each transformation.

TOOLS AND ESSENTIALS FOR SUCCESS

Starting a successful container garden requires a green thumb and a well-equipped arsenal of essential tools. Let's explore the importance of each tool and when and how they are used:

Containers

Containers are the foundation of any container garden, and choosing the right ones is paramount. The importance of containers lies in their role as the vessel that houses and nurtures your plants. They also contribute to the aesthetic appeal of your garden, serving as a canvas for creativity and design. They can be chosen to complement your overall garden theme or add a decorative touch to your living space. When selecting containers, consider size, material, and drainage factors. Larger containers provide more room for root development and water retention, while proper drainage holes prevent waterlogged soil.

When and How to Use Containers

Use containers when you are ready to start your container garden or when transplanting or repotting plants. Fill containers with potting soil, plant your seeds or seedlings, and

water them adequately. Place containers in suitable locations based on the sunlight requirements of your plants.

Fertilizer

Fertilizer is the lifeblood of a thriving container garden, providing essential nutrients that may be depleted from the potting soil over time. The importance of fertilizer lies in promoting healthy plant growth, blooming, and fruiting. Container plants rely on the nutrients in their confined space, and regular fertilization ensures a continuous supply of the elements necessary for their well-being. Different fertilizers cater to various plant needs, ranging from slow-release granules for long-term nutrition to liquid fertilizers for quick absorption. Understanding the specific requirements of your plants and providing them with the appropriate nutrients is vital to a successful container garden.

When and How to Use Fertilizer

Apply fertilizer at specific stages of plant growth, typically during the growing season. Different fertilizers may have different application schedules, so follow product instructions. Apply fertilizer to the soil surface or mix it into the potting soil before planting. For established plants, carefully follow the recommended dosage and application method. Avoid direct contact between fertilizer and plant stems or leaves, and water the plants after application to help nutrients reach the roots.

Gardening Gloves

Gloves are essential in protecting your skin from potential injuries, irritants, or thorns you may encounter while handling soil, plants, or containers. Gloves offer a barrier against dirt and prevent blisters, cuts, or allergic reactions that can occur during prolonged gardening sessions. Choosing the correct type of gloves depends on the tasks at hand; sturdy gloves with reinforced fingertips may be suitable for heavy-duty activities like potting, while lightweight and breathable gloves are ideal for delicate tasks such as pruning or harvesting.

When and How to Use Gardening Gloves

Wear gardening gloves when engaging in hands-on activities, including planting, weeding, pruning, or handling soil and fertilizers. Wear gardening gloves to protect your

hands from dirt, thorns, and potential irritants. Choose gloves appropriate for the task, whether heavy-duty work like digging or delicate tasks like transplanting seedlings.

Potting Soil

Potting soil is the fundamental growing medium for container plants, and its importance cannot be overstated. Unlike garden soil, potting soil is specifically formulated for use in containers, providing a well-balanced mix of nutrients, aeration, and water retention.

The significance of potting soil lies in its ability to support plant roots, facilitate drainage, and prevent compaction. It acts as a reservoir for nutrients and water, ensuring your container plants have the ideal growing conditions. When starting a container garden, choosing a high-quality potting mix tailored to the specific needs of the plants you intend to grow is crucial.

When and How to Use Potting Soil

Use potting soil to fill containers for planting. Whether transplanting seedlings or potting mature plants, potting soil is the essential medium. Fill your containers with potting soil, leaving sufficient space for the roots of your plants. Gently firm down the soil to eliminate air pockets without compacting it too much. Ensure the soil level is appropriate for the specific plants you're cultivating.

Seed Starting Medium

Seed starting medium, often called seed starting or soilless mix, is a specialized growing medium designed to provide an optimal environment for seed germination. Unlike regular garden soil, seed starting medium is lightweight, well-aerated, and sterile, minimizing the risk of diseases that can impede germination. The importance of using a seed starting medium lies in its ability to offer the right balance of moisture retention and drainage, creating an ideal foundation for seeds to sprout and establish healthy root systems.

When and How to Use Seed Starting Medium

Seed starting medium is used when germinating seeds indoors or in a controlled environment before transplanting seedlings into larger containers. Fill seed trays or individual containers with the seed starting mix, plant the seeds at the recommended depth, and keep the medium consistently moist until germination occurs. The lightweight

nature of the mix ensures that emerging seedlings can quickly push through the surface for their first touch of light.

Seed-Starting Trays

Seed-starting trays are designed to hold individual cells or compartments, providing an organized and efficient way to germinate multiple seeds simultaneously. The importance of seed starting trays lies in their ability to simplify the seed germination process, promote uniform growth, and facilitate the eventual transplanting of seedlings into larger containers. The trays also aid in proper spacing, preventing overcrowding that can lead to resource competition among seedlings.

When and How to Use Seed-Starting Trays

Seed-starting trays are used during the early stages of seed germination. Fill each cell with a seed-starting medium, plant the seeds, and provide the necessary conditions for germination. Once the seedlings have developed true leaves and are ready for transplanting, they can be easily removed from the trays, minimizing disturbance to their delicate roots.

Trowel

A trowel is a handheld digging tool with a pointed blade, and its importance in container gardening lies in its versatility for various tasks. Trowels are essential for digging, transplanting, and manipulating soil in containers. The sturdy design allows for efficient soil movement and ensures that planting or repotting is done precisely, minimizing root disturbance.

When and How to Use a Trowel

A trowel is used when planting seeds or seedlings, transplanting established plants into larger pots, or adjusting the soil level in containers. Its pointed end aids in creating planting holes, while the flat blade facilitates efficient soil scooping. The ergonomic handle ensures a comfortable grip during extended gardening sessions.

Watering Can

Adequate and precise watering is fundamental to the success of container gardening, making watering an indispensable tool. A watering can deliver a controlled and targeted flow of water directly to the base of plants, avoiding water wastage and minimizing the risk of overwatering or underwatering.

When and How to Use a Watering Can

A watering can is used throughout the container gardening process. It is employed to keep the seed starting medium consistently moist during germination, water seedlings as they grow, and maintain the hydration of mature plants. The spout of the watering can allow for an accurate pour, ensuring that water reaches the roots where it is needed most.

Hand Cultivator

The hand cultivator is a small, three-pronged tool for cultivating, loosening soil, and removing weeds. Its importance lies in its efficiency in breaking up compacted soil in containers, ensuring proper aeration, and facilitating the incorporation of fertilizers or soil amendments. The hand cultivator's compact size makes it ideal for maneuvering in tight container spaces.

When and How to Use a Hand Cultivator

Use the hand cultivator when preparing the soil for planting in containers. Gently rake the soil surface with the prongs to break up clumps, remove debris, and create a loose, well-aerated foundation for your plants. It can also be employed for light weeding between plants without disturbing their roots.

Pruner or Garden Shears

Pruners or garden shears are essential for maintaining the health and shape of your container garden. They allow you to accurately trim and prune plants, remove dead or diseased foliage, and shape the overall appearance of your garden, promoting healthy growth.

When and How to Use Pruners or Shears

Pruners are used throughout the growing season to trim back spent blooms, prune unruly branches, and shape plants for optimal aesthetics. Ensure clean cuts to minimize stress on plants and reduce the risk of disease transmission. Regular pruning also enhances air circulation, reducing the likelihood of fungal issues.

Kneeling Pad

Gardening often involves extended periods of kneeling or sitting, and a kneeling pad provides essential comfort and support, reducing strain and discomfort during planting, weeding, and other gardening tasks.

When and How to Use a Kneeling Pad

Use a kneeling pad whenever you engage in tasks that require kneeling or sitting. Place it on the ground to provide a comfortable and supportive surface for your knees, or sit on it while working at ground level. The pad protects your joints and enhances your overall gardening experience.

Plant Supports

As plants grow, some may require additional support to prevent them from sprawling or bending under their weight. Plant supports, such as stakes or cages, are crucial for structural support. The importance of plant supports lies in their ability to promote upright growth, prevent breakage, and enhance the overall appearance of your container garden.

When and How to Use Plant Supports

Use plant supports as your plants mature and begin to exhibit sprawling tendencies. Install stakes or cages near the base of the plant and gently secure stems to prevent them from leaning or breaking. This is particularly important for tall or top-heavy plants to maintain a tidy and upright posture.

Plant Labels

Plant labels are vital for maintaining organization and record-keeping in your container garden. The importance of plant labels lies in their role in identifying different plants, tracking planting dates, and recording specific care instructions. This organized approach facilitates effective management of your container garden and allows you to track the success and growth of each plant.

When and How to Use Plant Labels

Attach plant labels when planting to keep track right from the start. Mark each container with the plant's name, variety, and relevant information, such as planting dates or specific care requirements. This ensures that you can easily differentiate between different plants and maintain a comprehensive record of your container garden.

In the upcoming chapters, we will delve into the nuances of selecting suitable types of plants for your container garden and explore the intricacies of soil choices.

Understanding these aspects will further empower you to create a thriving and bountiful container garden that reflects your unique gardening vision.

ASK YOURSELF THESE QUESTIONS

- What is the unique microclimate of your urban space in terms of sun, shelter, and heat reflection?
- Considering temperature, how might excessive heat affect your plants, especially in small spaces?
- What are your goals for container gardening? For example, beauty, self- sufficiency, enjoyment, health, wildlife attraction, sustainability.
- What is your ideal number of pots, balancing effort and reward?
- Where is the nearest water source for efficient watering?
- What are your preferred edible plants, considering your and your family's tastes?

IN SUMMARY

- Container gardening is a versatile horticultural practice that involves cultivating plants in containers rather than traditional ground beds.
- Container gardening is space-saving and allows for a greater variety of plants.
- Containers serve as versatile design elements, enhancing the overall landscape or home decor.
- Container gardens offer you more control over the elements, diseases, pests, and weeds.

- Essential tools and supplies ensure successful container gardening, from containers and soil to watering cans and pruning tools.
- Organizational elements like plant labels contribute to the effective management and tracking of your container garden.

IN THE NEXT CHAPTER

Now that we have learned a little more about the art of container gardening, it is time to learn about the canvas on which gardeners do their work. In the following chapter, we will look at how to identify and access available spaces, find out how to choose suitable containers, and explore some different vegetables and flowers ideal for container gardening and companion planting.

2

PLANNING: SPACES, CONTAINERS AND PLANTS

THE SUCCESS STORY OF OWL CHILD CARE SERVICES

After receiving a grant from Seeds of Diversity Canada, John Sweeney of Owl Child Care Services expanded their existing garden, created a picnic area for the children, and built a garden shed to store their gardening supplies and tools safely.

The children were excited to participate in the project and eagerly helped build the raised bed, then decorated it and planted a wide range of vegetables. They enjoyed it immensely and learned much from their thriving garden, even inviting their parents to partake in the harvests.

Just like the children from Owl Care Child Services were excited about the project, your kids will need little encouragement to get their hands dirty in the garden, especially when it is easily accessible. Why not make it a family garden and get everyone involved in planning, planting, and growing fresh, beautiful plants?

ASSESSING YOUR SPACE

Before choosing plants and containers, you must evaluate the available space. Take measurements of the designated area for your container garden to ensure the selection of appropriately sized containers and plants.

A few additional factors need to be considered when assessing your space: the sun's role in your garden, the physical area you have available for containers, the location of your water source, and whether you will need to use vertical space.

Understanding the Sun's Impact on Plants

The sun powers plant growth through photosynthesis, converting sunlight into energy for various metabolic functions. To ensure your plants get enough sunlight, consider the following things:

- **The six-hour rule:** Most plants flourish with about six hours of daily sunlight. Observe your garden's sunlight duration and intensity, noting plant preferences for strategic placement.
- **Morning vs. afternoon sun:** As the sun travels across the sky, the angle at which its light reaches your plants changes throughout the day. The morning sun suits

plants desiring a softer touch, while the afternoon sun benefits those thriving in higher light levels. Observe patterns to position plants accordingly.

- **Detecting shadows:** Note shadows from nearby structures, trees, or buildings, indicating obstructed sunlight. Plan placement of shade-tolerant plants or arrange containers to minimize shadow impact.
- **Sun-loving and shade-tolerant plants:** Plants vary in sunlight preferences. Full-sun plants need at least six hours of direct sunlight, while partial-sun or dappled-shade plants thrive with three to six hours of bright light. Match plant varieties to your garden's light conditions.
- **Seasonal variations:** Sunlight patterns shift with seasons as Earth orbits the sun. Understand these variations to plan a garden for year-round success.

Physical Space

Even though container gardening allows you to grow plants practically anywhere, assessing all the available space is important. Let's explore why taking measurements is essential and how it contributes to effective utilization:

- **Container placement:** Measure your space to strategically position containers, ensuring organized and aesthetically pleasing arrangements. This guarantees each container receives enough light and fresh air.

- **Preventing overcrowding:** Measuring your space helps allocate enough room between containers, preventing overcrowding and competition for resources, as well as issues like poor air circulation and increased disease susceptibility.
- **Tailoring container selection:** Assessing your space influences container choice, ensuring a seamless fit into the designated area. Whether small pots on a windowsill or larger containers on a patio, accurate measurements help you better plan the space and prevent overwhelming it.
- **Accommodating growth and accessibility:** Consider plant growth when measuring. Make sure your plants have enough space for foliar growth or expansion. Plan for accessibility so you can move containers around comfortably for tasks like watering, pruning, and harvesting without damaging your plants or creating obstacles.
- **Customizing layouts for aesthetics:** Measuring enables a customized layout aligned with your vision. Accurate measurements contribute to the overall visual appeal, whether symmetrical, tiered, or a mix of sizes.
- **Adapting to environmental factors:** Consider sunlight and wind direction when assessing. Understanding environmental interactions helps position containers strategically, creating microclimates for the right balance of sunlight and protection from winds.

Water Sources

Having a water source near your garden can significantly improve your watering routine. Let's explore its importance and contributions to successful gardening:

- **Critical for the hydration of plants:** Being close to a water source simplifies watering and provides plants with the moisture they need to perform essential functions such as nutrient absorption and overall growth.
- **Efficient watering routine:** Close water access enables an efficient watering routine, which is of the utmost importance during dry or hot weather for maintaining soil moisture and preventing stress and damage to your plants.
- **Time and effort savings:** Nearby water saves time and effort, especially as your garden grows, streamlining the watering process.
- **Adaptability to container gardening:** Critical for container gardening, immediate water access addresses the specific needs of potted plants in limited soil volumes.
- **Consistent watering schedule:** Consistency is vital; nearby water makes keeping to a regular watering schedule easier, promoting stable soil moisture levels.
- **Watering accessibility for all plants:** Tailor watering based on plant needs, with different plants having varying water requirements, promoting nuanced care.

- **Environmental considerations:** Close water access encourages responsible water usage, facilitating practices like rainwater collection or drip irrigation.
- **Your comfort and enjoyment:** Enhancing the overall gardening experience, nearby water promotes fun and creativity, freeing you from logistical challenges.

CHOOSING THE RIGHT CONTAINERS

With the dizzying array of available containers, choosing the right ones can be a little overwhelming. Selecting the proper containers is essential to provide the perfect conditions for your plant's health and the overall success of your garden.

Thrillers, Spillers, and Fillers

Creating a beautiful container garden can be as easy as following this three-step formula:

1. **The thriller:** This is the plant and container that will be the focal point of your garden. You can make it even more eye-catching by elevating the thriller using a pedestal or a trellis.
2. **The spiller:** Your spiller plants should be allowed to grow over the edge of their containers. Creeping plants and ground covers make excellent spillers.
3. **The filler:** Plants with small leaves and flowers are great for filling in the rest of the spaces in the container. Make sure to use perennials or plants that will fill the space for the duration of the growing season.

Consider the following factors when choosing containers:

Size

The size of the container directly impacts the space your plants have to expand their roots into.

- Larger plants like pumpkin, peppers, tomatoes, root vegetables like carrots, and long radish varieties need deeper containers to spread their roots.
- Large containers help prevent root binding, which limits nutrient absorption and hampers plant growth. Ensure containers provide sufficient space for root systems to expand.
- Larger containers retain moisture longer, benefiting plants requiring consistent hydration. Their size also offers insulation, regulating soil temperature and preventing root stress in extreme weather.
- Smaller containers dry out faster and may need more frequent watering. Their temperatures may fluctuate widely, which could lead to plant stress.

Shape

The shape of the container not only contributes to garden aesthetics but influences how the roots will grow.

- Tall containers encourage longer vertical roots and are suitable for deep-rooted plants. Wide, shallow containers promote lateral root growth for spreading plants.

- Round pots allow maximum exposure to sunlight, but plants may develop roots that circle the circumference of smaller round pots, which may lead to absorption issues. Square pots have more volume than round pots and may retain moisture longer.
- Tall, cylindrical containers add vertical interest, while broad, squat ones offer a grounded appearance.

Color and Pattern

Container color and pattern enhance visual appeal and influence soil temperature.

- A container's color can impact the soil temperature. Dark containers absorb heat, which is beneficial in cooler climates but risky in hot regions.
- Light-colored containers reflect sunlight, keeping the soil cooler and increasing available light for photosynthesis, especially in low-light conditions.
- Container color and pattern enhance visual appeal. Vibrant colors create a lively atmosphere, while neutral tones offer a more serene backdrop. Patterns complement the environment.

Materials

Containers vary in materials, each with unique advantages. Your containers' material contributes to many factors, from moisture retention to insulation against temperature fluctuation.

- Porous materials such as terracotta or fabric pots provide aeration and contribute to the container's drainage and aeration. Glazed terracotta, ceramic, plastic, and metal containers retain moisture for longer and are good choices for plants needing consistent moisture.
- Insulating materials like thick ceramic protect roots from temperature extremes, which is vital in regions with fluctuating weather.
- Consider container weight, especially if you'll need to move them often. Lightweight plastic containers can easily be moved around. Heavy terracotta, stone, or ceramic containers are stable and won't topple easily but require more effort to move.
- For outdoor gardens exposed to direct sunlight, opt for UV-resistant containers. This will ensure many years of use while being exposed to sunlight without becoming brittle or discolored. Select weather-resistant containers for harsh elements. Materials should withstand intense sunlight, strong winds, or freezing temperatures to ensure longevity and the well-being of your plants.

Other Considerations

- **Drainage holes:** Prevent waterlogged soil and root rot by selecting containers with drainage holes. If a favorite container lacks drainage, consider adding more holes. Also, consider raising the containers slightly off the ground to ensure that the drainage holes are not obstructed and that water can drain away freely.
- **Aesthetic appeal:** Containers contribute to garden aesthetics. Choose designs that complement your garden style, experimenting with shapes, colors, and textures.
- **Compatibility with plant types:** Choose containers aligned with your plant's preferences. Succulents thrive in well-draining containers, while ferns prefer those retaining more moisture.

ECO-FRIENDLY CONTAINERS AND MATERIALS

Choosing eco-friendly or biodegradable plant pots benefits the environment, plant health, and gardening convenience, aligning with broader efforts to reduce the ecological footprint. It also educates gardeners about sustainable gardening, fostering environmentally conscious choices.

The demand for eco-friendly products drives industry innovation, leading to new materials and technologies aligned with sustainability on the market.

Biodegradable Containers

Unlike other materials, biodegradable pots break down, offering a range of benefits:

- Biodegradable pots allow air and water permeability, perfect for natural root development and healthier plants.
- These pots break down naturally, minimizing the environmental impact of using plastic. They decompose into organic matter, reducing long-term waste.
- Directly planting seedlings and their pots into the soil minimizes disturbing roots and transplant shock, promoting seamless integration.
- Made from bamboo, coconut coir, or molded fiber, these pots reduce reliance on finite resources, promoting sustainable practices.
- Compostable pots can be included in compost heaps or municipal composting systems, facilitating responsible disposal while reducing the burden on landfills.

Reusable Containers

- Some pots retain moisture, aiding water management, which is especially beneficial in arid climates or for moisture-sensitive plants.
- Some are made from recycled and recyclable materials, reducing waste and creating a circular economy.

PLANT SELECTION

Achieving well-balanced plant combinations in your garden requires knowing which plants work well together and which pairings should be avoided.

Tips for Good Plant Combinations

- **Complementary growth habits:** Pairing plants with similar growth habits will prevent competition resources. For example, combine low-growing groundcovers with taller, upright plants to create a visually appealing layered effect.

- **Consider bloom times:** Choose plants that bloom at different times to maintain continuous color in your garden throughout the growing season. This way there will always be something in bloom.
- **Texture and foliage contrast:** Create dynamic combinations by pairing plants with contrasting textures and foliage. Combine fine-textured plants with bold, coarse ones to add visual interest and depth to your garden.
- **Complementary colors:** Choose plants with colors that complement each other to establish a unified and visually appealing color scheme. Understanding color theory can guide you in choosing plants that enhance each other when placed side by side.
- **Functional pairings:** Practice companion planting for practical benefits, such as deterring pests or enhancing soil fertility. For example, plant aromatic herbs like basil or rosemary near vegetables to repel pests.
- **Consider sun and water needs**: Pair plants that need the same amounts of sunlight and water together. This ensures that all plants in a particular area receive the necessary light and moisture for optimal growth.
- **Beneficial attractors:** Include plants that attract beneficial insects, such as pollinators or predators of garden pests. For example, planting marigolds can attract pollinators, while dill attracts beneficial insects that prey on harmful pests.

- **Companion planting for vegetables:** In vegetable gardens, practice companion planting to enhance growth and repel pests. For instance, planting tomatoes with basil can improve the flavor of tomatoes and deter certain pests.

Combinations to Avoid

- **Competing for resources:** Avoid planting species that compete heavily for water, nutrients, light, or space. Make sure the plants have enough room to grow without overcrowding.
- **Incompatible sunlight needs**: Be mindful of the sunlight preferences of each plant in the combination. Avoid pairing sun-loving plants with those that thrive in shade to prevent one from suffering unless the sun-loving plants provide shade for the shade plants.
- **Disease and pest vulnerability:** Keep in mind the susceptibility of plants to common diseases and pests. Avoid pairing plants that are prone to the same issues to prevent widespread infestations.
- **Differing watering needs:** Plants with vastly different watering needs may struggle when sharing the same container. Avoid combining succulents with water-loving plants to prevent overwatering issues.
- **Invasive species**: Be cautious with plants that are known to be invasive or aggressive in their growth habits. Research each plant's behavior to prevent one species from dominating the container.

- **Soil pH compatibility:** Some plants prefer acidic soils, while others thrive in alkaline conditions. Avoid combining plants with drastically different soil pH requirements to ensure optimal growth.
- **Allelopathic plants:** Some plants release chemicals that inhibit the growth of nearby plants. Research and avoid combinations that include allelopathic species to promote healthy growth.

PLANTING ESSENTIALS

Choosing the best planting practices will help you to create thriving and visually appealing container gardens. Experiment, observe, and adjust based on your plant's needs, and most importantly, enjoy the journey of nurturing your container garden.

Choose the Right Container

- **Why**: Containers should be large enough to support the plant's root system, they must have drainage holes to prevent waterlogged soil, and they should match the aesthetic you have in mind for your garden's design.
- **How**: Pick pots with drainage and consider the material they are made of.

Select Quality Potting Mix

- **Why**: Good soil provides essential nutrients, aeration, water retention, and drainage for plant roots without introducing pests, weeds, or pathogens.
- **How**: Use a well-draining, lightweight potting mix designed for container gardening; avoid garden soil for better results.

Consider Plant Placement

- **Why**: Different plants have varied sunlight needs.
- **How**: Place sun-loving plants where they get direct sunlight and shade-loving ones in shaded areas.

Mind Watering Needs

- **Why**: Overwatering or underwatering harms plants by preventing essential metabolic processes from happening.
- **How**: Feel the soil; water when the top inch is dry. Adjust the watering frequency based on plant needs.

Fertilize Wisely

- **Why**: You might need to feed container plants more often than plants in traditional gardens, as container soil has fewer natural processes to produce nutrients than natural soil.

- **How**: Use a balanced, water-soluble fertilizer or slow-release fertilizers during the growing season. Always follow the instructions provided on the package.

Group Plants Smartly

- **Why**: Grouping plants by their water, light, and pH needs will simplify care.
- **How**: Place together plants with similar requirements for efficient watering and maintenance.

Prune and Deadhead

- **Why**: Removing old flower stalks and branches encourages new growth and keeps plants looking neat.
- **How**: Trim dead or yellowing leaves and remove spent flowers regularly.

Mulch for Moisture Retention

- **Why**: It reduces evaporation, keeping the soil consistently moist for longer.
- **How**: Apply a layer of organic mulch, like bark or compost, on the soil surface.

Support Tall Plants

- **Why**: It will prevent branches and stems from bending or breaking in strong winds.
- **How**: Stake or use plant supports for taller plants, securing them to prevent toppling. Ideally, stakes should be put in place at the time of planting to disturb the plant's roots.

Rotate and Rearrange

- **Why**: This will ensure even sunlight exposure and prevent one side from getting leggy.
- **How**: Turn containers occasionally and rearrange as needed for balanced growth.

Plan for Seasonal Changes

- **Why**: Plants may have different needs in each season.
- **How**: Swap out seasonal plants, provide shading or coverings, adjust watering, and fertilize according to seasonal requirements.

Regularly Inspect and Refresh Soil

- **Why**: Soil compacts over time, affecting aeration.
- **How**: Periodically refresh soil by removing the top layer and replacing it with fresh potting mix or topping up containers with compost and working it into the top inch or two of the soil.

Be Mindful of Plant Size

- **Why**: Prevent overcrowding and competition for resources.
- **How**: Research mature sizes; give each plant enough space to grow without crowding others. When plants are potted individually, they can be spread out as the plants grow larger.

Enjoy the Process

- **Why**: Gardening is rewarding and therapeutic.
- **How**: Take time to observe and enjoy the growth of your container garden. Celebrate successes and learn from challenges. Explore new plants and planting methods.

SUCCULENTS

Planting and maintaining succulents in container gardens can be a rewarding and visually appealing way to enjoy these unique, low-maintenance, and resilient plants. Here is a step-by-step guide on the basics of planting and caring for succulents in containers:

- **Choose the right container:** Select containers with drainage holes to prevent waterlogged soil, as succulents are susceptible to root rot. Containers made of materials like terracotta or unglazed ceramics are preferable, as they allow for better airflow.

- **Use well-draining soil:** Use a well-draining potting mix specifically formulated for succulents or amend regular potting soil with perlite or sand. This helps prevent water retention, maintaining the ideal moisture balance for succulents.
- **Select healthy succulents:** Choose healthy succulents with vibrant colors and firm leaves. Avoid plants with signs of pests, disease, or etiolation—stretching and yellow coloration due to insufficient light. Ensure that the selected succulents have similar sunlight and water requirements.
- **Prepare the container:** Fill the container with the prepared, well-draining soil, leaving enough space at the top for the plants. Gently tap the container on a flat surface to settle the soil and remove air pockets.
- **Plan the arrangement:** Before planting, arrange the succulents in the container to visualize the design. Consider the growth habits and colors of each succulent for an aesthetically pleasing arrangement.

- **Planting procedure:**

  - Gently loosen the roots and remove the plants from their pots. If the roots are compacted, you can tease them apart to encourage outward growth.
  - Dig shallow holes in the soil for each succulent. Ensure the plants are planted at the same depth as

they were in their original pots.
  ○ Place the succulents in the prepared
    holes, backfilling with soil and
    gently pressing it down to secure
    the plants.

- **Water after planting:** Water the succulents lightly after planting to settle the soil. Follow a "soak and dry" watering schedule. Allow the soil to dry out completely before the next watering, as overwatering is a common issue with succulents.
- **Sunlight requirements:** Place the container in a location where the succulents receive plenty of sunlight. Most succulents thrive in bright, indirect light, or direct sunlight for a few hours each day. Adjust the exposure based on the specific needs of the succulent species.
- **Temperature considerations:** Succulents generally prefer warm temperatures. Protect them from frost and extremely low temperatures, especially if they are sensitive species. Consider moving containers indoors during colder months if necessary.
- **Fertilizing:** Fertilize only when it's the growing season. Use a balanced, diluted succulent fertilizer and follow the recommended application rates on the product label. Avoid over-fertilizing, as succulents generally have low nutrient requirements.

UNDERSTANDING HARDINESS ZONES: MATCHING PLANTS TO YOUR CLIMATE

Hardiness zones, as defined by the USDA, indicate the climatic conditions of a region, primarily based on winter temperatures. Understanding hardiness zones ensures a more informed and successful gardening experience. It serves as a valuable guide for selecting plants that can withstand extreme temperatures and the typical climatic

conditions of your region, ultimately contributing to the health and longevity of your garden.

Importance of Hardiness Zones

Climate compatibility: Different zones experience varying temperature ranges. Selecting plants suitable for your zone ensures they can thrive in your local climate.

Survivability: Plants adapted to your zone are more likely to survive winter lows and summer highs, reducing the risk of loss due to extreme weather.

Choosing Plants for Your Zone

Research local conditions: Understand the specific characteristics of your zone, such as average frost dates and temperature ranges.

Selecting plants: Opt for plants recommended for your zone, considering their cold hardiness and heat tolerance.

Popular Plants by Zone

- **Zone 3–4 (Northern US, Canada):** Spruce trees, lilacs, and cold-hardy vegetables like cabbage and carrots.
- **Zone 5–6 (Midwest US):** Plants: Roses, tomatoes, and perennials like daylilies.
- **Zone 7–8 (Southern US, Coastal areas):** Crepe myrtles, magnolias, and heat- tolerant herbs like rosemary.
- **Zone 9–10 (Florida and the southern parts of Louisiana, Texas, California, and Arizona):** Citrus trees, hibiscus, and tropical plants like orchids.

Adapting to Microclimates

Microclimates within a zone can result from factors like urban heat or sheltered areas. Adjust plant choices based on these variations.

Plant Hardiness Guides

- **Local resources:** Consult local nurseries, garden centers, or agricultural extension offices for plant guides tailored to your region.
- **Online tools:** Visit sites https://planthardiness.ars. usda.gov for online plant hardiness zone maps and databases for detailed information.

Zone Considerations for Container Gardens

- **Flexibility**: Containers provide some flexibility, allowing you to experiment with plants slightly outside your zone.
- **Winter protection:** Move containers to sheltered areas or insulate them during extreme cold.

Zone Changes Over Time

Due to climate change, zones may shift. Stay updated on revised hardiness maps to adapt your plant selections.

THE BEST PLANTS FOR CONTAINER GARDENS

Some plants grow too prolifically for containers and small spaces and may not be able to reach maturity before they become unwieldy and take over the little space you have.

The following is a general guide to some of the most popular plants that are suitable for container gardens:

Fruits

Strawberries: Ideal for hanging baskets or containers, strawberries offer sweet berries and don't require much space.

Dwarf citrus trees: Lemons, limes, or oranges can thrive in pots, providing fresh citrus in limited spaces.

Vegetables

Tomatoes: Compact varieties like cherry or patio tomatoes are excellent for containers. Ensure proper support for vertical growth.

Peppers: Perfect for pots, peppers are colorful and can be grown in sunny locations.

Carrots: Shorter carrot varieties suit shallower containers well, and their unique colors add visual appeal.

Lettuce and spinach: Leafy greens are well-suited for shallow containers, and they grow fast, allowing for continuous harvesting.

Flowers

Marigolds: These vibrant flowers are easy to grow and help deter pests, making them a great addition to container gardens.

Petunias: Cascading or compact petunias provide a burst of color and are low- maintenance.

Geraniums: With various colors, geraniums thrive in pots and attract pollinators.

Herbs

Basil: A versatile herb that adapts well to containers, basil enhances various dishes and can be grown indoors or outdoors.

Rosemary: Resilient and aromatic, rosemary is well-suited for larger pots, providing a steady supply for culinary use.

Mint: Plant mint in containers to control its spreading nature. It's great for teas, cocktails, and culinary uses.

Chives: Compact and onion-flavored chives are easy to grow in smaller pots.

Personal Preferences

Plant what you love: Tailor your container garden to include plants you enjoy cultivating and consuming.

Aesthetic appeal: Consider the visual harmony of plant combinations, selecting varieties that complement each other.

PLANTING CALENDAR

Vegetables

Note that vegetables should not be planted or transplanted from October 1st to February 15th unless you are starting seedlings indoors, in which case you can plant them several weeks in advance and transplant them once the threat of frost has passed.

Vegetables	Days to Harvest	Jan	Feb	Mar	Apr	May	June	July	Aug
Green Beans	50-70				From the 15th: Seeds	All Month: Seeds	All Month: Seeds	Until the 15th: Seeds	
Beets	55-60		From the 15th: Seeds	All Month: Seeds					All Month: Seeds
Carrots	75-80		All Month: Seeds					From the 15th: Seeds	Until the 15th: Seeds
Cucumbers	60-65				From the 15th: Seeds and Transplants	Until the 15th: Seeds and Transplants			From the 1st until the 15th: Seeds and Transplants
Snap Peas	65-70		All Month: Seeds						
Peppers	50-60					All month: Transplants			
Summer Squash	50-60				From the 15: Transplants	Until the 15th: Transplants			
Swiss Chard	60-70			From the 15the: Seeds and Transplants	All month: Seeds and Transplants				

Fruit

Note that most fruit trees will only bear edible fruit a few years after planting.

Fruit	Jan	Feb	Mar	Apr	May	June	July	Aug	Sept	Oct	Nov	Dec
Blueberry	All Month: Plant	All Month: Plant				All month: Harvest	All month: Harvest	All month: Harvest		All Month: Plant	All Month: Plant	All Month: Plant
Citrus				From the 15th: Plant	All month: Plant		From the 15th: Harvest	All month: Harvest	All month: Harvest	All month: Harvest	All month: Harvest	
Fig	All month: Plant	All month: Plant	All month: Plant				All month: Harvest	All month: Harvest	All month: Harvest	All month: Harvest		All month: Plant
Grape		From the 15th: Plant	All month: Plant	All month: Plant			From the 15th: Harvest	All month: Harvest	All month: Harvest	All month: Plant	Until the 15th: Plant	
Strawberry					All month: Harvest	Until the 15th Harvest				From the 15th: Plant	Until the 15th: Plant	

Herbs

Note that the window for planting or transplanting most herbs is from February 15th to May 15, with the exception of parsley, which can be transplanted again during September.

Herbs	Harvest Season	Jan	Feb	Mar	Apr	May
Basil	Summer				All month: Transplants	Until the 15th: Transplants
Chamomile	Late summer to early fall				From the 15th: Seeds	Until the 15th: Seeds
Chives	Spring to fall				All month: Transplants	Until the 15th: Transplants
Cilantro	Early summer		From the 15th: Seeds	All month: Seeds		
Lavender	Summer			All month: Transplants	Until the 15th: Transplants	
Oregano	Summer to fall			All month: Transplants	Until the 15th: Transplants	
Parsley	Summer to fall				All month: Transplants	Until the 15th: Transplants
Rosemary	Year-round				All month: Transplants	Until the 15th: Transplants
Sage	Summer to fall				From the 15th: Transplants	Until the 15th: Transplants
Thyme	Summer			From the 15th: Seeds and Transplants	All month: Seeds and Transplants	Until the 15th: Seeds and Transplants

IN SUMMARY

- Evaluate the space you have available by taking measurements and choosing appropriate containers.
- Most plants need 6 hours of sun every day. Take note of the changing angle of sunlight during the day and position plants accordingly.
- Allocate enough room between containers to prevent issues like poor air circulation and plants competing for sunlight.
- Grow plants upwards on walls, trellises, or support structures to maximize gardening space.

- Choose plants like tomatoes, cucumbers, and peas that naturally grow vertically for efficient use of space.
- Having a nearby water source simplifies watering, saving time and effort.
- Keep 'thrillers, spillers, and fillers' in mind when designing your garden and choosing plants and containers.
- Select containers based on plant size. Allow enough room to accommodate the plant's spreading roots.
- Use quality potting mix for best results, and avoid using gardening soil.
- Pair plants with similar habits and practice companion planting.

IN THE NEXT CHAPTER

Now that we have taken a look at how to assess the available space in your garden, covered the topic of containers and their features, and learned about planting essentials and hardiness zones, we can dive into the role of soil and selecting the best medium for your plants, as well as sustainable gardening practices to reduce your carbon footprint.

3

SOIL HEALTH AND ECO-FRIENDLY GARDENING TECHNIQUES

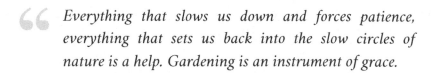

Everything that slows us down and forces patience, everything that sets us back into the slow circles of nature is a help. Gardening is an instrument of grace.

— MAY SARTON

THE ROLE OF SOIL

Soil serves as a vital medium for the growth of plants and trees, providing physical support by anchoring the plant, as well as a reservoir for essential nutrients and water. The air between soil particles supplies plants' roots with the oxygen they need to function. Soil is a complex ecosystem comprising minerals, organic matter, water, air, and a diverse community of microorganisms. The composition and health of the soil play a pivotal role in determining the success of your container garden.

WHAT NUTRIENTS NEED TO BE PRESENT IN THE SOIL AND WHY?

Practically all types of soil contain various levels of nutrients in the form of organic matter and minerals. We'll now look at the essential elements, how they affect the growth of plants, and the signs plants display when the soil contains these elements in excess and when it is deficient in them.

Major Elements

Plants require the major elements in relatively large quantities for proper growth and development. Together, the three main elements, nitrogen (N), phosphorus (P), and potassium (K) are known as NPK. Bags of fertilizer will usually display the NPK ratio of

the contents. The other major elements are calcium (Ca), magnesium (Mg), and sulfur (S).

Trace Elements

Plants need these elements in smaller amounts. While they are equally crucial for plant health, the quantities required are minimal compared to the major elements. Examples of trace elements include iron (Fe), manganese (Mn), copper (Cu), zinc (Zn), boron (B), and molybdenum (Mo).

Nitrogen

Plants use nitrogen to produce enzymes, proteins, and chlorophyll. It promotes vigorous vegetative growth, enhances leaf and stem development, and improves plant health.

- **Excess**: Initially, excessive nitrogen can result in vigorous vegetative growth, lush foliage, and dark green leaves. Prolonged excess nitrogen can lead to imbalanced growth, leaf burn, delayed flowering, and increased susceptibility to pests and diseases. It may also impact the quality of fruits and flowers.
- **Deficiency**: Nitrogen deficiency manifests as stunted growth, yellowing (chlorosis) of older leaves, and reduced overall plant vigor. It adversely affects protein synthesis and other essential processes.

Phosphorus

Phosphorus is Involved in energy transfer, photosynthesis, and the formation of DNA and RNA. It stimulates root development, aids in flowering and fruiting, and enhances plant energy transfer processes.

- **Excess**: Phosphorus toxicity is uncommon in natural conditions but can interfere with trace element uptake. It may lead to deficiencies of other elements.
- **Deficiency**: Phosphorus deficiency results in poor root development, delayed flowering, and reduced fruiting. Leaves may exhibit a purplish tint, and overall growth is

stunted. Phosphorus is crucial for energy transfer in plants.

Potassium

Potassium regulates water uptake, enzyme activation, and carbohydrate metabolism. It improves drought tolerance, enhances disease resistance, and promotes disease susceptibility, plant vigor, and stress tolerance.

- **Excess**: Excessive potassium can interfere with the uptake of other nutrients, leading to imbalances. It may cause magnesium and calcium deficiencies.
- **Deficiency**: Potassium deficiency results in weak stems, poor drought tolerance, and increased disease susceptibility. Leaves may show yellowing along the leaf margins and exhibit scorching or browning.

Calcium

Calcium is essential for cell wall formation, membrane structure, and enzyme activation. It promotes strong cell walls, improves plant structure, and helps prevent disorders like blossom end rot in fruits.

- **Excess**: Excessive calcium is rare but can lead to imbalances with other cations. It may interfere with the uptake of magnesium and potassium.
- **Deficiency**: Calcium deficiency causes blossom end rot in fruits, stunted root growth, and distorted leaves. It is

crucial for cell wall structure and integrity. Plants may exhibit necrosis and increased vulnerability to diseases.

Magnesium

Magnesium is a constituent of chlorophyll, which is essential for photosynthesis. It enhances photosynthesis, improves nutrient uptake, and contributes to overall plant energy metabolism.

- **Excess**: Excessive magnesium is rare and typically not harmful to plants. It may lead to imbalances with other nutrients, like calcium, affecting their uptake.
- **Deficiency**: Magnesium deficiency results in yellowing between leaf veins (interveinal chlorosis), starting in older leaves. It affects chlorophyll production, photosynthesis, and overall plant energy transfer.

Sulfur

Sulfur is a component of amino acids, vitamins, and coenzymes. It Supports protein synthesis, aids in root development, and contributes to forming essential compounds.

- **Excess**: Sulfur excess is uncommon but can occur in areas with acid rain. It may lead to imbalances with other nutrients, affecting plant health.
- **Deficiency**: Sulfur deficiency causes yellowing of young leaves, stunted growth, and reduced protein

synthesis. It impacts the plant's ability to produce essential amino acids and vitamins.

Iron

Iron is essential for chlorophyll synthesis and enzyme activation. It prevents chlorosis, enhances photosynthesis, and promotes plant health and vigor.

- **Excess**: Excessive iron can lead to iron toxicity, resulting in leaf bronzing, leaf tip burn, and reduced root growth. It interferes with the uptake of other essential nutrients.
- **Deficiency**: Iron deficiency causes interveinal chlorosis in young leaves. It affects chlorophyll production, leading to poor photosynthesis and overall growth. Plants may exhibit a yellowing appearance.

Manganese

Plants need Manganese to breathe, photosynthesize, and for nitrogen metabolism. It supports chlorophyll production, activates enzymes, and contributes to plant growth and development.

- **Excess**: Excessive manganese can result in toxicity symptoms, such as leaf discoloration, brown spots, and reduced growth. It interferes with the uptake of other nutrients.

- **Deficiency**: Manganese deficiency leads to interveinal chlorosis in young leaves, similar to iron deficiency. It affects photosynthesis, enzyme activation, and overall plant vigor.

Copper

Copper is involved in various enzymatic reactions. It supports plant metabolism, aids in photosynthesis, and contributes to overall plant health.

- **Excess**: Excessive copper can contaminate plants, leading to wilting, leaf distortion, and reduced growth. It interferes with iron uptake and may harm beneficial microorganisms in the soil.
- **Deficiency**: Copper deficiency results in stunted growth, chlorosis (yellowing) of leaves, and distorted shoot tips. It affects various enzyme activities critical for plant metabolism.

Zinc

Zinc activates enzymes and regulates hormones. It promotes overall plant growth, aids in seed formation, and enhances stress tolerance.

- **Excess**: Excessive zinc can lead to zinc toxicity, causing leaf chlorosis, reduced growth, and interference with iron and manganese uptake. It may result in imbalances with other nutrients.

- **Deficiency**: Zinc deficiency causes interveinal chlorosis in young leaves, stunted growth, and distorted leaf development. It impacts enzyme activities involved in various metabolic processes.

Boron

Plants need Boron for carbohydrate metabolism and cell division. It facilitates flower and fruit development, enhances nutrient uptake, and supports overall plant reproductive processes.

- **Excess**: Excessive boron is toxic to plants, leading to leaf burn, necrosis, and reduced growth. It interferes with nutrient uptake and disrupts cell wall formation.
- **Deficiency**: Boron deficiency results in distorted and discolored young leaves, stunted root and shoot growth, and poor flower and fruit development. It affects cell division and membrane integrity.

Molybdenum

Molybdenum is essential for nitrogen metabolism and enzyme activation. It facilitates nitrogen fixation in legumes, supports plant nitrogen utilization, and enhances overall plant health.

- **Excess**: Excessive molybdenum is rare but can lead to molybdenum toxicity, causing chlorosis, reduced growth, and nutrient imbalances. It may interfere with nitrogen metabolism.

- **Deficiency**: Molybdenum deficiency causes interveinal chlorosis in older leaves, reduced nitrogen fixation in legumes, and impaired enzyme activities. It affects plant nitrogen utilization.

SOIL SELECTION

Selecting the right soil is perhaps the most critical choice you can make for your container garden to ensure healthy plants and vigorous growth. Let's take a look at what you should look for in good container garden soil:

Types of Soils

Potting soil: This is a common choice for container gardening. It is specifically formulated for potted plants, providing a well-balanced mix of peat or coconut coir, compost, vermiculite, and perlite. Look for options with added organic matter for nutrient retention.

Garden soil: Garden soil from your backyard can be used as a cheap amendment to potting soil but may contain pathogens and be too dense for container gardening when used on its own. It's recommended to amend garden soil with organic matter and perlite for improved drainage.

Succulent mix: Ideal for succulents and cacti, this mix has enhanced drainage properties to prevent waterlogged soil.

Seed starting mix: Light and sterile, this mix is suitable for germinating seeds in containers. It promotes healthy seedling development up to the transplant stage.

What Soil to Use

Well-draining mixes: Opt for soils that facilitate good drainage, preventing soggy conditions that can lead to root rot. This is crucial for most plants, especially those susceptible to overwatering.

Nutrient-rich options: Look for soils enriched with organic matter or slow-release fertilizers. These provide essential nutrients for plants throughout the growing season.

pH-balanced soils: Some plants have specific pH preferences. Testing and adjusting the soil pH or selecting a pH-neutral mix can benefit plants with particular requirements.

Sterile mixes: To minimize the risk of soil-borne diseases and pests, choose sterile mixes for container gardening.

What Soil Not to Use

Topsoil: Pure topsoil does not contain many space nutrients, tends to be too dense for container gardening, and may lack the necessary aeration and drainage. Topsoil should be used as a soil amendment or part of a soil mix to reap its benefits.

Garden soil: Using garden soil without amendments can lead to compacted and poorly draining soil.

THE COMPLETE CONTAINER GARDENING HANDBOOK | 75

Soil from unknown sources: Avoid using soil collected from unknown or contaminated sources, as it may introduce pests, diseases, or weed seeds to your garden.

How Much Soil is Needed

Consider container size: The volume of soil required depends on the size of the container. Larger containers need more soil but provide adequate root growth space and better moisture retention.

Filling depth: Fill containers with enough soil to accommodate the root depth of the chosen plants. As a general guideline, leave a couple of inches at the top to allow watering without the soil spilling over.

Compactness: Light, fluffy mixes may settle over time, so it's advisable to slightly overfill initially and to top up containers to compensate for settling.

SUSTAINABLE CONTAINER GARDENING PRACTICES

By incorporating these sustainable container gardening practices, you can create gardens that provide aesthetic pleasure and contribute to the environment's and local ecosystems' overall health.

Embracing sustainable practices in container gardening contributes to ecological well- being and promotes a harmonious relationship between home gardens and the environment.

Permaculture

Encourage a more natural, overgrown landscape to benefit wildlife and beneficial insects. Allowing wildness in your garden can create habitats for pollinators and other fauna.

Promote a diverse range of plant species to enhance ecosystem resilience. Companion planting and creating mini-ecosystems within containers contribute to a balanced, self- sustaining garden.

No Dig Gardening

Adopt a no-dig approach to preserve soil structure and microbial life in your containers. You maintain a healthy soil ecosystem by not disturbing the soil once it has settled.

Peat-Free Gardening

Opt for coco coir instead of peat-based products. Coco coir is a sustainable alternative made from coconut husks, a by-product of the coconut industry. Using coco coir reduces the ecological impact associated with peat extraction.

Reusing Pots and Upcycling Materials

Extend the life of plastic pots by reusing them for multiple plantings. This minimizes plastic waste and supports a circular economy.

Repurpose old or discarded materials for constructing garden structures. Upcycling materials like wooden pallets, old crates, or broken terracotta pots reduces waste and adds a unique aesthetic to your garden.

You can reuse potting soil for a few years as the organic matter in them breaks down slowly. Avoid reusing potting soil that insects or soil-borne pathogens may have contaminated.

Organic Pest Control

Implement natural pest control methods, such as introducing beneficial insects or using companion plants that repel pests. This reduces the need for chemical pesticides, promoting a healthier garden ecosystem.

Oils such as neem, rosemary, and peppermint are natural deterrents of various garden pests.

Community Engagement

Engage with local gardeners and the community to share knowledge and experiences about sustainable gardening practices. Collaborative efforts can strengthen the impact of sustainable gardening on a broader scale.

REDUCING YOUR ENVIRONMENTAL FOOTPRINT

Reducing the environmental footprint in container gardening involves mindful practices that contribute to sustainability. Here are ways you can achieve this:

Reduce Fertilizer Usage

- Use slow-release or organic fertilizers instead of synthetic fertilizers to minimize the frequency of applications.
- Employ compost or well-rotted manure to enhance soil fertility naturally.
- Do soil tests to determine specific nutrient needs, allowing for targeted and efficient fertilizer use.

Reduce Water Consumption

- Implement water-efficient irrigation methods, such as drip irrigation or soaker hoses to minimize water wastage, implement to minimize water wastage.
- Mulch the soil surface to retain moisture, reducing the frequency of watering.
- Collect rainwater in barrels for irrigation to reduce dependence on treated water. Note that regulations regarding rainwater collection differ from region to region, so check your local laws before investing in rainwater harvesting systems.

Source Plants Locally

- Purchase plants from local nurseries or growers to reduce transportation-related carbon emissions.
- Choose native or locally adapted plant species better suited to the regional climate, reducing the need for excessive watering and care.

Take Care of Your Gardening Tools

- Regularly clean and maintain gardening tools to extend their lifespan, reducing the need for frequent replacements.
- Choose durable, high-quality tools that are less likely to contribute to waste through breakage or wear.

Capture Carbon

- Integrate carbon-capturing plants into container gardens, such as certain succulents and ornamental grasses. Perennial plants capture more carbon than annual ones.

- Implement composting practices to recycle kitchen waste, providing nutrient-rich soil amendments while reducing your overall carbon footprint.
- Choose containers made from sustainable materials like recycled plastic or bamboo, contributing to reduced carbon emissions in the production process.

Making Compost

- Instead of throwing out kitchen scraps, lawn trimmings, and leaf matter, collect them in a composter or compost heap.
- Paper and cardboard are biodegradable and can serve to bulk up your compost. We will be looking at how to make compost in the following chapters.

IN SUMMARY

- Soil composition and health play an essential role in gardening success.
- Plants require the major elements (N, P, K, Ca, Mg, and S) in larger quantities than the trace elements (Fe, Mn, Cu, Zn, B, and Mo)
- Potting soil is suitable for most plants in container gardening because of its organic material content and its good balance of drainage and water retention.

- Avoid using garden soil in container gardening.
- Reduce your environmental footprint by using organic, slow-release fertilizers or compost.
- Reduce water usage by mulching, using drip irrigation, and collecting rainwater.
- Use local plant species better adapted to your region for greater success.
- Use containers made of sustainable materials.
- Reuse old gardening materials, such as plastic pots and potting soil, and upcycle old materials for your garden.
- Use sustainable gardening practices such as permaculture or no-dig gardening to promote biodiversity in your garden.

IN THE NEXT CHAPTER

Now that we've looked at what makes healthy soil and learned about a few eco-friendly gardening techniques, we will be looking at design principles to spruce up small spaces, learn how to expand your growing space and maximize harvests by practicing vertical gardening, and look at a few simple DIY techniques to get you growing.

4

DESIGNING YOUR CONTAINER GARDEN

> *The single greatest lesson the garden teaches is that our relationship to the planet need not be zero-sum and that as long as the sun still shines and people still can plan and plant, think and do, we can, if we bother to try, find ways to provide for ourselves without diminishing the world.*

— MICHAEL POLLAN

DESIGN PRINCIPLES FOR SMALL SPACES

Designing container gardens in small spaces involves a thoughtful application of color, shape, texture, form, focal points, line, proportion, scale, balance, and contrast. Understanding and implementing these design principles allows even the smallest spaces to transform into vibrant and visually captivating container gardens.

Color

Color is a fundamental and powerful element that significantly influences the aesthetic and emotional impact.

How color functions in garden design:

- **Hue**: The primary color itself is referred to as the hue. Hues include variations of primary colors—red, blue, and yellow—and secondary colors—green, orange, and purple—as well as all the shades and tones in between.
- **Color wheel:** The color wheel is helpful for understanding color relationships. It categorizes colors into primary, secondary, and tertiary hues, simplifying the creation of harmonious color schemes.

  - *Analogous colors*: Colors adjacent to each other on the color wheel create a harmonious and serene effect.
  - *Complementary colors:* Colors opposite each other on the color wheel provide strong contrast and vibrancy.

- **Warm colors:** Reds, oranges, and yellows evoke energy, vibrancy, and warmth. They tend to advance visually, making spaces feel more intimate and inviting.
- **Cool colors:** Blues, greens, and purples are calming, creating a sense of tranquility. They recede visually and can make spaces feel more expansive.

- **Monochromatic colors:** Variations in lightness and saturation of a single color, creating a sophisticated and unified look.
- **Seasonal variation:** Plants often contribute to the garden's color palette, and their blooms can change with the seasons. Understanding the seasonal progression of colors allows for dynamic and ever-changing garden displays.
- Limit the color palette to create a cohesive and uncluttered look. Choose a few complementary colors to establish a theme and tie the design together.

Shape

Shape refers to the external outline or form of elements within the garden, such as plants, structures, pathways, and decorative features. The shape of these elements contributes significantly to the visual impact and structure of the garden.

How shape functions in garden design:

- **Plant forms:** Tall, vertical plants create a sense of height and add vertical interest to the garden.
- **Spreading or horizontal shapes:** Plants with a spreading habit cover more ground horizontally and can be used to create a ground cover or define boundaries.
- **Round or mounded shapes:** Plants with a rounded or mounded form add softness and visual appeal. They are

often used as focal points or to create a sense of balance.

- **Containers and planters:** The shape of containers, pots, or planters contributes to the design. Varied container shapes add interest, and their placement can influence the garden's layout.
- **Symmetry and asymmetry:** Symmetrical shapes create a formal and balanced look, while asymmetrical arrangements can be more dynamic and informal.
- **Diversity**: Incorporate a diverse mix of plant shapes and structures. Varying the forms of plants, such as combining trailing vines with upright flowers, adds visual interest and depth to your garden.

Texture

Texture refers to the visual and tactile surface characteristics of plants, hardscape elements, and other features within the garden. Texture adds depth, interest, and a sensory dimension to the design.

How texture functions in garden design:

- **Fine texture:** Plants with small leaves or delicate foliage create a fine texture. They often appear soft and provide a sense of intricacy and detail.
- **Medium texture:** Plants with moderate-sized leaves contribute a balanced and versatile texture to the garden.

- **Coarse texture:** Plants with large, bold leaves or a robust structure create a rough texture. They add a strong visual presence and can become focal points.
- **Smooth texture:** Plants with smooth, glossy, or shiny leaves have a sleek and refined appearance.
- **Rough texture**: Plants with textured or fuzzy leaves provide a more tactile experience and can create a more casual or natural look.
- **Tactile elements:** Including plants or features that invite touch enhances the sensory experience of the garden.

Form

Form refers to plants' overall shape and structure, hardscape elements, and other features within the garden. It encompasses the three-dimensional aspect of the garden and influences the visual impact, style, and functionality of the space.

How form functions in garden design:

- **Upright/formal:** Plants with an upright and formal form have a vertical, symmetrical structure. They are often used to create a sense of order and architectural design.
- **Weeping/informal:** Plants with a weeping or informal form have a more relaxed and cascading structure. They add a softer, more naturalistic feel to the garden.
- **Round/ball-shaped:** Plants with a round or ball-shaped form provide a sense of symmetry and balance.

They are often used as focal points or for creating structured arrangements.

- **Linear forms:** Straight lines and geometric shapes in hardscape elements, such as pathways or raised beds, contribute to a formal form. This style is often associated with more structured and organized designs.
- **Curves**: Curved lines and organic shapes in hardscape elements create an informal form. This design style is softer and often mimics the natural flow of the landscape.
- **Structural form:** Architectural features like pergolas, arbors, or trellises contribute to the overall form of the garden. They provide vertical elements and define spaces within the landscape.
- **Layered form:** Incorporating plants and features with varying heights and depths creates a layered form. This adds visual interest and depth to the garden.
- **Adapt to site conditions:** Consider the natural contours and topography of the site. The form of garden elements should complement and work with the existing conditions.

Focal Points

Focal points are prominent and strategically placed elements that draw attention and become central to the overall garden layout.

Establish focal points using plants, statues, fountains, and ornaments with unique shapes, vibrant colors, or interesting textures. These focal points draw attention and create visual interest within the limited space.

Focal points can change with the seasons. For example, a flowering tree might be a focal point in spring, while a sculpture takes the spotlight in winter.

The selection and placement of a focal point depend on the style and size of the garden and your personal preferences. A well-chosen focal point contributes to the garden's overall harmony and visual appeal, making it a memorable and enjoyable space.

Line

A line refers to the eye's visual path as it moves through the landscape. Lines are fundamental elements that contribute to a garden's overall structure, movement, and organization. They are crucial in shaping the design, directing attention, and creating a sense of flow. Consider the direction of plant growth and how lines can create movement or direct attention to focal points.

How line functions in garden design:

- **Straight lines:** Straight lines convey a sense of formality and order in the garden. They are often associated with geometric designs, formal layouts, and structured environments.

- **Architectural elements:** Straight lines are common in features like pathways, fences, and raised beds. They contribute to a clean and organized appearance.
- **Curved lines:** Curved lines create a more naturalistic and informal feel in the garden. They mimic the organic flow of nature and soften the overall design.
- **Diagonal lines:** Diagonal lines introduce a dynamic and energetic quality to the garden. They create movement and visual interest, making the design more engaging.
- **Horizontal lines:** Horizontal lines convey a sense of stability and tranquility. They are often associated with features like retaining walls, terraces, or low plantings close to the ground.
- **Vertical lines:** Vertical lines draw the eye upward and emphasize height. Tall plants, trees, or vertical structures contribute to a sense of verticality and can create a feeling of enclosure.
- **Combining curves:** Combining curves with other line types adds complexity and interest to the garden. This approach allows for a more varied and visually engaging design.
- **Implied lines:** Implied lines are not physically present but are suggested by the arrangement of elements. For example, the alignment of stepping stones may create an implied path, guiding movement.

Proportion

Proportion refers to the harmonious relationship between the different elements within a landscape. It involves balancing various components' size, scale, and visual weight to create a visually pleasing and cohesive overall design. Proportion is crucial in achieving balance, symmetry, and unity in the garden.

How proportion functions in garden design:

- **Scale**: Scale addresses the relative sizes of different elements in relation to each other and the overall space. For example, the size of plants, structures, and hardscape features should be proportional to the garden size.
- **Consideration of growth:** Proportion involves considering the eventual size of plants at maturity. Planting choices should align with the available space to prevent overcrowding or the dominance of certain elements.
- **Layering heights:** Planting of varying heights contributes to a sense of depth and proportion. Taller plants at the back or center can provide a backdrop for shorter plants in the foreground. Ensure that taller plants do not overpower smaller ones.
- **Complementary sizing:** The size of a focal point should be proportionate to its surroundings. It should stand out but not disrupt the overall balance of the garden.

Scale

Scale refers to the relative size of various elements within the landscape in relation to each other and to the overall space. It involves carefully considering and balancing the size of plants, structures, hardscape features, and decorative elements to create a visually harmonious and proportionate garden.

How scale functions in garden design:

- **Proportional harmony:** Scale ensures that the sizes of different elements are proportionate, creating a harmonious relationship. It helps avoid extremes, such as overly large or small features, contributing to a balanced and aesthetically pleasing design.
- **Plant size:** Scale is significant when selecting and arranging plants. The height of plants at maturity should be considered to prevent overcrowding or the dominance of certain species. Tall plants, medium-sized shrubs, and ground cover should be strategically placed to achieve balance.
- **Structures and hardscape:** Elements like patios, pathways, pergolas, and other structures should be scaled appropriately for the size of the garden. Oversized or undersized structures can disrupt the overall design. For instance, a large, elaborate structure may overwhelm a small garden.
- **Consistency**: Maintaining a consistent scale in plant size, spacing, and structural elements contributes to a cohesive and unified appearance.

Balance

Balance in garden design refers to the distribution and arrangement of elements within the landscape to create visual stability and harmony. There are two main types of balance in garden design:

- **Symmetrical balance:** Arranging elements in a mirrored or evenly distributed pattern on either side of a central axis creates a formal and organized appearance. For example, if a large tree is planted on one side of a garden, a similar tree may be planted on the opposite side to maintain symmetry.
- **Asymmetrical balance:** Asymmetrical balance, also known as informal balance, is achieved by arranging different elements to create equilibrium without mirroring each other. This approach relies on visual weight rather than identical shapes. For instance, a large, visually striking plant on one side of a garden may be balanced by several smaller, less conspicuous plants on the opposite side.

Contrast

Contrast refers to the juxtaposition of different elements, such as colors, shapes, sizes, textures, or forms, to create visual interest and highlight the unique characteristics of each component. It involves strategically placing diverse elements to enhance their individual qualities and make the overall garden more dynamic and appealing. Contrast adds excitement, depth, and variety to the landscape.

How contrast functions in garden design:

- **Color contrast:** Using contrasting colors can be visually striking. For example, pairing complementary colors (those opposite each other on the color wheel, like red and green) creates vibrant and energetic combinations. Contrasting light and dark colors or warm and cool tones adds visual interest.
- **Texture contrast:** Contrast in texture involves combining plants or materials with different surface qualities. Pairing fine-textured plants with bold, coarse ones or integrating smooth surfaces with rough ones creates tactile diversity. This is particularly effective in close-up or touchable areas of the garden.
- **Form and shape contrast:** Varying the shapes and forms of plants or garden structures contributes to contrast. For instance, pairing tall, upright plants with low, spreading ones creates a dynamic silhouette. Mixing different shapes, such as round and spiky, adds visual excitement.
- **Size and scale contrast:** Contrasting the sizes of plants or garden features helps create a sense of scale. Mixing large and small elements strategically prevents monotony and fosters a more engaging visual experience. This is crucial in avoiding a uniform or cluttered appearance.

- **Light and shadow contrast:** Contrasting areas of light and shadow can highlight specific elements. Placing plants with varying heights or textures in areas with different light exposure creates visually appealing contrasts in illumination.

Design Tips to Maximise Your Garden Space

1. **Keep it simple:** When dealing with limited space, simplicity is key. Opt for clean lines and uncluttered arrangements. Avoid overcrowding your containers

with too many plants or intricate decor. A minimalist approach makes maintenance more manageable.

2. **Design using foliage and bold details:** Emphasize the beauty of foliage to add visual interest. Choose plants with diverse leaf shapes, sizes, and textures to create a dynamic and engaging container garden. Intersperse these with bold details such as vibrant flowers or unique containers. This combination adds depth and character to your small space.

3. **Enclose the space to block visual distractions:** Consider creating a defined space for your container garden. This can be achieved by using trellises, screens, or strategically placed larger plants. Enclosing the area helps to block out visual distractions from the surroundings, creating a more intimate and focused environment.

4. **Play with color palettes and textures**: Explore the visual impact of color and texture in your container garden. Choose a cohesive color palette to unify the design, and play with contrasting textures for added interest.

5. **Consider tiered planting:** Introduce depth and dimension by incorporating tiered planting in your small space. Use shelves, plant stands, or tiered containers to create vertical layers. This also adds an interesting visual aspect.

DIY SPACE OPTIMIZATION IDEAS

Assess Your Space and Determine Your Goals

Before diving into vertical gardening, assess your available space and establish your goals. Consider factors such as sunlight, accessibility, and the aesthetic you want to achieve. This initial step sets the foundation for a successful vertical garden.

Maximize Vertical Space

Vertical gardening involves making the most of your vertical space to grow plants. Here are several creative ideas to achieve this:

Wall-mounted planters: Install planters directly onto walls. These can be individual pots, pockets, or modular systems that allow plants to thrive vertically. This method transforms bare walls into vibrant green spaces.

Hanging planters: Suspend planters from the ceiling or other structures to create an eye-catching display. This is particularly useful for trailing or cascading plants that benefit from the vertical descent.

Shelving units: Incorporate shelves to hold a variety of plant containers. This tiered approach maximizes space and adds an organized and visually appealing element to your vertical garden.

Ladder plant stands: Repurpose a ladder as a plant stand. Each step becomes a platform for pots, allowing plants to ascend in an organized and stylish manner.

Plant walls or living walls: Create a living work of art by installing a plant wall. This involves using a vertical framework to host a variety of plants, turning any surface into a lush and vibrant garden.

Window shelves: Use windowsills as additional space for small potted plants. This optimizes sunlight exposure and enhances the view from both inside and outside.

Tension rod planters: Install tension rods strategically and hang planters from them. This method is adjustable and ideal for spaces with limited floor area.

Stacking planters: Opt for stacking planters that allow you to grow multiple plants vertically. These are designed to stack securely, providing a compact solution for growing herbs, flowers, or vegetables.

VERTICAL GARDENING

A vertical garden is a gardening technique where plants are grown on vertically inclined structures instead of traditional horizontal beds. This method allows for the cultivation of plants in a more space-efficient and visually striking manner. By understanding the concept of vertical gardening and its associated benefits, you can explore this innovative technique to enhance your gardening experience, even in limited spaces.

The benefits of vertical gardening include:

- **Space optimization:** Vertical gardens efficiently use limited space, making them ideal for small balconies, patios, or urban environments where horizontal space is scarce.
- **Aesthetic appeal:** Vertical gardens add a decorative element to indoor and outdoor spaces. They can serve as living art, enhancing the visual appeal of walls, fences, or other vertical surfaces.
- **Improved air circulation:** Vertical gardening offers the advantage of enhanced air circulation, which prevents conditions conducive to mold and mildew growth, which thrive in damp environments.
- **Reduced pest issues:** Elevating plants can help deter certain pests and diseases that may affect ground-level gardens. This can contribute to healthier and more resilient plant growth.
- **Accessibility and maintenance:** Vertical gardens can be designed at various heights, making accessing and maintaining plants easier.
- **Versatility and creativity:** Vertical gardening allows for creative arrangements and combinations of plants. Gardeners can experiment with different plant species, colors, and textures to create unique and personalized designs.

DIY VERTICAL GARDENING TECHNIQUES

When implementing these DIY vertical gardening techniques, consider the specific needs of your plants, including sunlight, water, and spacing requirements. Experiment with different arrangements and plant combinations to achieve a visually appealing and functional vertical garden that suits your available space and style preferences.

Tiered Planters

Tiered planters involve arranging containers at different heights, creating a vertical cascade of plants. This technique not only maximizes vertical space but also allows for a variety of plants with different light and water requirements to coexist. You can use various materials, such as wooden crates, metal stands, or repurposed pallets to create a tiered effect.

Arbors

Arbors serve a dual purpose as both a vertical structure and a support for climbing plants. Consider planting climbing or vining plants like ivy, roses, or beans that can gracefully cover the arbor, providing shade and visual interest.

Shoe Organizer

Repurposing a shoe organizer into a vertical garden is a creative and budget-friendly option. Hang the shoe organizer on a wall or over a door, and fill each pocket with soil to create individual planting pockets. This method works well for growing herbs, small flowers, or succulents.

Wall Planters

Wall planters are specifically designed containers that can be mounted on walls or fences, transforming vertical surfaces into planting areas. These planters come in various designs, materials, and sizes, offering flexibility in arranging plants vertically.

They are suitable for both indoor and outdoor spaces, providing an opportunity to create a living wall filled with greenery.

TIPS FOR STARTING A VERTICAL GARDEN

- Enhance your garden entrance with an arbor, adding both aesthetics and a vertical structure for climbers like roses or jasmine. Choose decorative and sturdy arbors that complement your garden.
- Opt for lightweight, mobile trellises for flexibility in arranging your vertical garden. Easily accommodate changes in sunlight or create different focal points with trellises made from materials like bamboo.
- Utilize existing fencing or rails for instant vertical planting space. Attach containers, hanging planters, or vertical plant pockets to maximize space and create a lush backdrop. Ensure the structure is sturdy enough for plant weight.

- Support plants with a natural, rustic aesthetic using sticks or branches as stakes. This cost-effective method is ideal for taller or climbing plants like tomatoes or beans, providing support without overshadowing natural beauty.

CREATING BEAUTIFUL CONTAINER GARDEN THEMES

Depending on the space you have available, consider the following ideas for utilizing the space:

- **Vertical designs:** Explore wall-mounted shelves, repurposed pallets, or specialized vertical garden systems to maximize vertical space.
- **Balcony designs:** Design your container garden to fit the limited space of a balcony, incorporating a mix of herbs, flowers, or even small fruit trees.
- **Indoor designs:** Create a charming indoor garden with compact containers featuring herbs, succulents, or aromatic plants to engage your senses.
- **Designs for small spaces:** Optimize limited spaces by using hanging baskets with trailing plants or choosing compact varieties of flowers and herbs.
- **Seasonal designs:** Tailor your container garden to the seasons, such as a salad greens planter for fresh produce or flowering plants for bursts of color.
- **Other creative ideas**: Explore unique themes like a mini desert garden with cacti, a fairy garden with

miniature accessories, or a sensory garden with
aromatic plants.

IN SUMMARY

- Warm colors like red, orange, and yellow evoke energy
  and warmth. Cool colors like blue, green, and purple
  are calming, creating a sense of tranquility.
- Symmetrical shapes evoke feelings of formality and
  balance, while asymmetrical arrangements feel more
  dynamic and informal.
- Texture refers to the visual and tactile surface
  characteristics of plants, hardscape elements, and other
  features within the garden.
- Form refers to the shape of plants, containers, and
  other features.
- Focal points are prominent and strategically placed
  elements that draw attention.
- Lines guide your eyes through the garden and create a
  sense of flow.
- Proportion is the relationship between the different
  elements within the garden.
- Scale is the relative size of various elements within the
  garden in relation to each other and to the overall
  space.
- Achieving balance involves carefully considering the
  placement of plants, structures, colors, and other
  features.

- Vertical gardening has numerous benefits, including maximizing your space and increasing yields.

IN THE NEXT CHAPTER

After reading this chapter, you must be eager to design your container garden and express yourself using containers, plants, and vertical gardening techniques. The principles of garden design will be your guide in creating a beautiful garden space to unwind in. Next, we will learn the sustainable and eco-friendly art of turning kitchen and garden waste into nutrient-rich compost.

5

COMPOSTING FOR CONTAINER GARDENS

> *The organic gardener does not think of throwing away the garbage. She knows that she needs the garbage. She is capable of transforming the garbage into compost, so that the compost can turn into lettuce, cucumber, radishes, and flowers again...With the energy of mindfulness, you can look into the garbage and say: I am not afraid. I am capable of transforming the garbage back into love.*
>
> — NHAT HANH

UNDERSTANDING THE ROLE OF COMPOSTING

Composting is a natural process that transforms organic materials into nutrient-rich humus, known as compost. This decomposition occurs through the activity of microorganisms like bacteria, fungi, and other decomposers. Composting is a sustainable and eco-friendly approach to managing organic waste, diverting it from landfills and turning it into a valuable soil conditioner.

Benefits of Composting

Nutrient-Rich Soil Amendment

Compost is a rich source of organic nutrients and the elements necessary to maintain plant and soil health. It enhances the fertility of soil and promotes robust plant growth.

It conditions soil and improves its structure, enhancing water retention in sandy soils and promoting drainage in clay soils, creating an optimal environment for plant roots to thrive.

Microbial Activity Enhancement

Compost introduces beneficial microorganisms to the soil, nurturing a thriving microbial community. This, in turn, supports various soil processes, including nutrient cycling and disease prevention.

Reduced Waste in Landfills

By diverting organic waste from landfills, composting contributes to waste reduction. Organic materials in landfills can generate methane, a potent greenhouse gas. Composting helps mitigate this environmental impact.

Water Conservation

Improved soil structure resulting from compost use enhances water retention. This reduces the need for frequent irrigation, contributing to water conservation.

Temperature Control

Compost insulates the soil and prevents rapid temperature fluctuations, which can damage roots or cause heat stress in your plants.

Erosion Control

Compost serves as a protective layer against soil erosion. Its ability to bind soil particles helps prevent runoff and soil loss due to wind or water, particularly in sloped or vulnerable areas.

Cost Savings

Composting kitchen scraps and yard clippings is a cost-effective way of producing compost at home. Using homemade compost eliminates the need for store-bought fertilizers and soil conditioners, resulting in cost savings for gardeners. It is a sustainable and cost-effective solution.

What Can You Compost?

By incorporating various organic waste materials, you can create a nutrient-rich compost that benefits your garden and reduces overall waste. Understanding the role of green and brown materials and achieving the right balance between them ensures optimal conditions for the microorganisms living within the compost. It is critical to producing nutrient-rich compost for your garden.

Green Materials

Green materials in composting refer to nitrogen-rich components. These materials are typically fresh, moist, and rich in proteins. They provide essential nutrients and moisture, promoting the growth of microorganisms responsible for breaking down organic matter.

Examples of green materials include:

- **Kitchen scraps:** Peels, cores, seeds, and other remnants from fruits and vegetables are suitable. Add citrus peels in moderation, as excessive amounts may slow composting.
- **Coffee grounds:** Used coffee grounds are an excellent nitrogen source, enhancing the compost's nutrient content.
- **Stale bread and cereal:** Small amounts of stale bread, crackers, or cereal can be added in moderation.
- **Green yard waste:** Fresh grass clippings, leaves, small twigs, and plant trimmings contribute nitrogen to the compost pile. Once trimmings become dry and brittle, they are considered brown material.
- **Manure**: Well-aged manure from cattle, poultry, or rabbits adds nitrogen and accelerates decomposition.
- **Hair and pet fur:** Hair from brushes or pet fur, free from chemicals or medications, is a good source of slow-releasing nitrogen. Hair takes up to two years to decompose in compost and aids in moisture retention until it has fully broken down. Although hair is dry, it is considered green as it contributes a lot of nitrogen.
- **Seaweed**: Rinsed and chopped seaweed contributes minerals and enhances compost structure.

Brown Materials

Brown materials are carbon-rich components. These materials are usually dry, dead plant matter. They provide structure to the compost, improve aeration, and balance the nitrogen-rich green materials.

Examples of brown materials include:

- **Dry leaves:** Fallen leaves from deciduous trees are an excellent carbon source.
- **Straw**: Straw or hay adds carbon to the compost pile.
- **Wood chips:** Small amounts of untreated wood chips or sawdust can be included.
- **Nutshells**: Shells from nuts like peanuts, walnuts, and almonds can be included.
- **Shredded paper and cardboard:** Unbleached paper and cardboard add carbon, aiding in moisture retention and aeration.
- **Brown yard waste:** Dried leaves, spent flowers, stalks, and disease-free dried plant materials from the garden can be composted.
- **Eggshells**: Eggshells provide calcium to the compost, balancing acidity and promoting healthy microbial activity. Prepare the eggshells by baking them in the oven at 356°F for 10 minutes, crushing them fine, then adding them to the compost—store eggshells separately until you have enough to cover a baking tray to save energy.

- **Tea bags:** Used tea bags, as long as they are made of natural fibers without staples or synthetic elements.
- **Wood ash:** Wood ash is rich in calcium, potassium, phosphorus, and magnesium. It is alkaline and can help balance the compost's pH if it has become acidic.

The Importance of Balancing Green and Brown

Understanding the role of green and brown materials and achieving the right balance is critical to producing nutrient-rich compost for your garden.

The ideal compost pile has a mix of approximately three parts green to two parts brown by volume. This balance ensures the composting process is efficient, with the microorganisms breaking down the organic matter and producing nutrient-rich compost. Other ratios will also produce compost but may take longer to decompose.

What You Should Not Compost

- Meat, dairy, and oil can attract pests and slow decomposition.
- Diseased plants or weeds with seeds.
- Pet waste—unless using a specialized composting system.

TYPES OF COMPOSTING SUITABLE FOR SMALL SPACES

Vermicomposting

Vermicomposting is a sustainable and efficient method of composting organic waste using worms, typically red wigglers (*Eisenia fetida*) or other composting worms. These industrious creatures break down kitchen scraps and other organic materials into nutrient-rich compost, known as vermicompost or worm castings. This process is well- suited for small spaces, making it an ideal composting solution for apartment dwellers, urban gardeners, or anyone with limited outdoor areas.

Benefits of Vermicomposting

- Vermicomposting offers an environmentally friendly and space-efficient way to convert kitchen scraps into valuable compost, providing an excellent nutrient source for your plants.
- **Nutrient-rich compost:** Vermicompost is a potent organic fertilizer rich in essential nutrients.
- **Reduced kitchen waste:** Vermicomposting significantly reduces the amount of waste sent to landfills.
- **Ideal for small spaces:** Suitable for apartment balconies, kitchens, or other limited areas.
- **Year-round solution:** This can be done indoors, allowing year-round composting.

Bokashi Composting

Bokashi composting is a Japanese method of fermenting organic waste in an airtight container using bokashi bran—a mix of beneficial microorganisms. The term "bokashi" translates to "fermented organic matter." Unlike traditional composting, bokashi works anaerobically, meaning it ferments without oxygen. This makes it an excellent option for indoor composting, especially in small spaces like apartments or kitchens.

Benefits of Bokashi Composting

- **Indoor composting:** Suitable for small spaces, including apartments.
- **Faster breakdown:** Fermentation speeds up the decomposition of organic matter.
- **Nutrient-rich end product:** Bokashi waste can enrich the soil with beneficial microorganisms.
- **Odor control:** The airtight system minimizes unpleasant odors associated with composting.
- **No turning required:** Low maintenance; no need to turn the compost.

Compost Tumblers

A compost tumbler is a rotatable cylindrical container mounted on a frame. This design facilitates the easy turning and mixing of compost materials, promoting aeration and accelerating composting. Compost tumblers come in various sizes and techniques, making them suitable for small-scale and larger composting needs.

Benefits of Compost Tumblers

- **Low maintenance:** Easy rotation simplifies turning the compost.
- **Quick decomposition**: Regular turning accelerates the composting process.
- **Aeration**: Improved aeration leads to better breakdown of organic matter.
- **Compact design:** Ideal for small spaces and can be placed on patios or balconies.
- **Reduced odor:** Tumblers with secure seals minimize odors and deter pests.

Electric Composters

Electric composters, also known as electric composting machines or units, are innovative devices designed to accelerate the composting process. Unlike traditional composting methods that rely on natural decomposition, electric composters use controlled environments and technology to speed up the breakdown of organic waste into nutrient-rich compost.

Benefits of Electric Composters

- **Rapid composting:** Electric composters significantly reduce the time required compared to traditional methods. Some units can produce compost in a matter of weeks rather than months.
- **Compact and space-efficient:** Electric composters are often compact and suitable for small spaces, making them ideal for urban or indoor composting. They eliminate the need for sizeable outdoor compost piles.
- **Year-round composting:** Since electric composters regulate temperature, composting can occur year-round, unaffected by external weather conditions.
- **Low odor emission**: Controlled environments in electric composters help minimize unpleasant odors associated with traditional composting. Some units have built-in filters to reduce odors further.
- **User-friendly:** Electric composters are designed to be user-friendly, requiring minimal manual effort. They often have simple controls for temperature settings and operation.
- **Efficient use of kitchen scraps:** Electric composters efficiently process kitchen scraps, including vegetable peelings, coffee grounds, and other organic waste generated in households.

Considerations

- Electric composters require electricity, so access to a power source is always necessary.
- Some models may have limitations on the types of materials they can process.

Community Composting

Community composting is a collaborative approach to waste management where community members come together to compost organic materials collectively. Unlike individual composting, which is done on a household level, community composting involves a shared space or facility where multiple households contribute their organic waste.

Benefits of Community Composting

- **Reduced landfill waste:** Diverting organic waste from landfills reduces the environmental impact of waste disposal.
- **Community**: Fosters a sense of community as residents work together towards a common goal.
- **Educational opportunities:** Provides educational opportunities on composting and sustainable waste management.
- **Nutrient-rich soil:** Generates nutrient-rich compost that can be used to enhance local soil quality.
- **Shared responsibility:** Distributes composting efforts among community members.

- **Space-efficient:** Ideal for individuals with limited space at home.
- **Educational**: Promotes environmental awareness and community engagement.

Tips for Successful Community Composting

- Coordinate with neighbors and establish a system for contributing waste.
- Adhere to community composting guidelines to ensure proper composting practices.
- Monitor the composting site regularly to address any issues promptly.
- Ensure everyone involved is aware of what is and is not compostable.
- **Educate yourself:** Understand the specific requirements and guidelines on how to compost.

Choosing the Right Method

Vermicomposting: Perfect if you have minimal outdoor space or live in an apartment. Ideal for households producing a moderate amount of kitchen waste. If you don't want the added responsibility of caring for worms, this might not be the best method for you.

Bokashi: Suitable for composting kitchen scraps, including meat and dairy, without the space requirements of traditional composting.

Compost tumblers: Ideal for small yards or balconies, offering a convenient and efficient way to compost kitchen and garden waste.

Electric composters: They offer an efficient and convenient solution if you want to compost in limited spaces or are seeking a faster composting process.

CREATING NUTRIENT-RICH COMPOST FOR CONTAINER PLANTS

Hot Composting

Hot composting involves creating conditions to maintain higher temperatures. Using this method accelerates the decomposition process, producing finished compost in weeks. Hot composting requires turning the compost pile regularly to maintain aeration and promote even decomposition.

How to do Hot Composting

1. Choose a suitable location for your compost pile or set up a bin. A bin helps contain the materials and facilitates the hot composting process. Ensure good aeration by layering coarse materials like sticks or straw at the bottom.
2. Collect brown and green materials to compost.
3. Alternate layers of brown and green materials, aiming for a balanced mix. Shred or chop large materials to speed up decomposition.

4. Maintain the proper moisture level. Periodically check moisture levels, especially during dry periods, and add water if needed.

5. Turn the compost regularly for hot composting to introduce oxygen and facilitate microbial activity. Use a pitchfork or compost aerator to turn the materials, ensuring even decomposition.

6. Hot composting generates heat as microorganisms break down the organic matter. Check the internal temperature of the pile using a thermometer for accuracy. Aim for temperatures between 130°F to 160°F for efficient composting.

7. Adjust the balance of browns and greens if the compost is too wet—add more browns or dry—add more greens. Achieving the right balance ensures good decomposition.

8. Hot composting typically takes four to six weeks. The compost is ready once the internal temperature stabilizes and the materials break down. Allow the compost to cure for two to four weeks before use.

Benefits of Hot Composting

- Rapid breakdown of materials.
- Destruction of weed seeds and pathogens due to high temperatures.
- Production of nutrient-dense compost.

Cold Composting

Cold composting relies on natural decomposition processes and typically occurs at lower temperatures. It is a slower, less labor-intensive process, often taking several months to a year for the materials to break down completely. Unlike hot composting, which involves managing temperature and frequently turning, cold composting allows microorganisms, fungi, and insects to break down the organic matter at their own pace.

Cold composting requires minimal turning or aerating of the compost pile. It is a more hands-off approach.

How to do Cold Composting

1. Choose an accessible location for the compost pile in your garden, or invest in a compost bin. Bins help contain the materials and provide a tidy composting space.
2. Collect brown and green materials to compost.
3. Start with a layer of coarse brown materials at the bottom for aeration— alternate layers of brown and green materials, maintaining a good balance. Shred or chop larger pieces for faster decomposition.
4. Water each layer as you build the pile, and keep the pile moist. Monitor moisture levels and adjust as needed to maintain an optimal environment for decomposition.

5. While cold composting doesn't require regular turning, occasional mixing can accelerate the process. Turn the compost heap every few weeks for best results.
6. Once the composted materials have broken down into a dark, crumbly texture, the compost is ready to use. Cold compost can be applied directly to container plants or mixed with potting soil for added fertility.

Benefits of Cold Composting

- Minimal effort and maintenance.
- Low labor requirements compared to hot composting.
- Gradual release of nutrients over time.

Tips for Successful Composting

- Alternate layers of green and brown materials for a well-balanced compost pile.
- Turn the compost regularly to provide oxygen for the decomposition process.
- Maintain proper moisture levels. The compost should be spongy and moist, not unlike a wrung-out sponge.
- Finely chopped or shredded materials decompose faster.
- Composting takes time, but the result is nutrient-rich soil for your plants.
- Consider the placement of your compost if you lack a backyard or balcony. Options include under the sink, in a hall cabinet, or by the door. Ensure regular turning

and layering of organic materials to effectively manage odors and maximize compost efficiency.

IN SUMMARY

- Composting is the sustainable process of allowing organic waste to break down into nutrient-rich compost.
- Composting is beneficial for you, your plants, and the general environment.
- Keep a ratio of three parts green waste to two parts brown waste.
- Do not compost meat, dairy, oil, diseased plants, or pet waste.
- There are many compact and easy-to-use composting methods to choose from.
- Cold composting is low-maintenance, but the organic matter breaks down slowly.
- The heat generated when hot composting requires more maintenance but will kill off any pathogens, weed seeds, and insects present in the compost pile.

IN THE NEXT CHAPTER

Now that you have learned how to turn your kitchen or garden waste into nutrient-rich compost, you will have less need for commercial fertilizers, saving you money while being sustainable. Next, we will delve into your plants' watering, light, and temperature needs and how to fulfill them.

6

LIGHT, TEMPERATURE, AND WATER

Gardens are not made by singing 'Oh, how beautiful' and sitting in the shade.

— RUDYARD KIPLING

All plants placed in a container should be appropriate for the specific conditions of the container or planter's location. While most plants typically require six to eight hours of sunlight daily, vegetables thrive when given at least eight hours. If the intended location for the container garden is in a shaded area, choose plants that can thrive in such conditions.

If you want to cultivate tropical plants, it's essential to use portable planters that can be moved indoors during cooler months. Using lightweight planters placed on wheeled dollies makes them easy to move when needed. Moreover, it's advisable to keep potted plants at a distance from walls and elevated off driveways, stone, or cement patios to prevent potential scalding and overheating caused by the reflected heat during hot months.

LIGHT AND TEMPERATURE REQUIREMENTS

Light and temperature are critical factors influencing the well-being of plants. Understanding and adjusting these factors based on the specific needs of your plants will contribute to a healthier and thriving indoor garden. Regular monitoring and adaptation to seasonal changes will help keep the environment optimal for your plants.

Light Intensity

Light intensity is a critical factor influencing plant growth, categorized as low, medium, or high depending on a plant's specific needs. Understanding and meeting these requirements are essential for optimal growth. Low-light plants, such as ferns, thrive in shaded areas, while high-light plants, like succulents, need intense sunlight.

Assessing each plant's light preferences ensures they receive the right intensity for photosynthesis and metabolic functions. Observing light patterns in your garden helps strategically position plants, preventing issues like inadequate sunlight or scorched foliage. Tailoring light intensity to plant needs is fundamental for a thriving and healthy garden.

Light Exposure

Light exposure, referring to the duration of time plants are bathed in sunlight, is crucial for photosynthesis, a process essential for plant growth. Different plants have varying sunlight needs, with most vegetables thriving in full sun. Understanding these requirements is key to a successful garden.

Assess each plant's need for daily sunlight and ensure they receive the appropriate exposure to foster healthy development. Monitoring sunlight patterns in your garden and strategically placing plants based on their light preferences is essential. Adequate light exposure ensures optimal photosynthesis, leading to robust, flourishing plants in your vegetable garden.

Directional Exposure

Directional exposure, considering the source of light, significantly influences plant growth. In the northern hemisphere, south-facing windows receive direct sunlight, while north-facing ones offer indirect light. This variance affects plant development. To promote balanced growth, rotate plants regularly, ensuring each side receives adequate exposure. This practice is crucial for preventing uneven growth patterns caused by directional light sources.

By optimizing directional exposure, plants can photosynthesize efficiently from all angles, contributing to their overall health and symmetry. Thoughtful rotation aligns with the natural sunlight patterns, fostering robust and well-proportioned growth in indoor or container plants.

Temperature

Temperature influences various physiological processes in plants, including germination, photosynthesis, respiration, and transpiration. Plants generally thrive in temperatures between 50–75°F; however, some species need specific temperatures to grow their best and may have different tolerances for extreme temperatures.

Extreme temperatures can stress plants, leading to wilting, leaf burn, or even death. In cold climates, container plants may suffer from frost damage, while in hot climates, they might experience heat stress and scorched leaves.

Consider seasonal temperature variations and select plants that thrive in your specific climate. Take protective measures like mulching, shading, or using insulating containers to mitigate temperature extremes. Monitoring and responding to temperature changes ensure that your container gardens provide an environment conducive to healthy plant growth, resulting in more productive green spaces.

THE IMPORTANCE OF PROPER WATERING

Adequate watering is vital for the health of your container plants. Let's take a look at why:

Keep Soil Moist, But Not Wet

Maintaining the right soil moisture is a cornerstone of successful gardening, especially in container gardens. Most plants prefer moist but not wet soil. The key to proper watering is to strike the correct balance for the specific species. Wet soil poses a threat to plant health by limiting oxygen availability to the roots, leading to root rot and other moisture-related problems.

Prevent Nitrogen Loss

When soil is saturated, it results in denitrification—the loss of plant-usable nitrogen from the soil. Anaerobic bacteria convert nitrate into a gaseous form, causing it to escape from the soil. This can deprive your plants of essential nutrients.

Regularly Dump Water-Catching Trays

Regularly dump the water in water-catching trays to prevent waterlogged soil. Standing water in trays can contribute to soil saturation, impacting the root health of your plants.

Frequent Watering for Container Plants

Container plants typically require more frequent watering compared to those in traditional in-ground gardens. The limited soil volume in containers means they can dry out faster. Ensure the soil remains consistently moist to a depth of one to two inches, adjusting your watering frequency in hot or cold weather or as needed to meet the specific needs of your plants.

Humidity

Humidity, the moisture content in the air, significantly influences plant well-being. Certain plants, notably tropical species, flourish in environments where the humidity has been raised. Maintaining optimal humidity levels can be achieved through practices such as misting, employing humidity trays, or strategically grouping plants together.

THE DIFFERENT TYPES OF WATERING METHODS

Proper watering is a cornerstone of successful gardening. Let's take a look at watering methods to understand when and how each is best employed:

Misting

Misting involves gently spraying water to create a humid microclimate around the plants, which is mainly ideal for tropical plant varieties requiring higher humidity levels. This technique mimics natural conditions, but it can be beneficial during dry seasons or indoor environments with low humidity.

However, caution is essential to prevent over-misting, as excessive moisture on leaves or soil may foster fungal problems. Striking a balance in misting practices ensures a conducive environment for plant growth, promoting optimal humidity without risking the onset of issues related to prolonged dampness, thereby maintaining a healthy and thriving plant ecosystem.

How to mist:

1. Install a misting system or use a trigger sprayer on its finest setting.
2. Spray a fine mist of water onto plant leaves. You don't want them dripping wet.

Humidity Trays

Humidity trays are shallow containers that humidify the air immediately above or in the vicinity of the plants.

How to use a humidity tray:

1. Take a shallow tray or a container and fill it with pebbles.
2. Fill the humidity tray with water until the water level is just below the top layer of pebbles.
3. Place the container and plant on top of the pebbles. The container shouldn't be able to wick water up from the tray. The water in the tray will now slowly evaporate, humidifying the surrounding air.

Watering Can

A watering can is one of the simplest ways of watering small gardens. It's effective for precise watering, helping to control and monitor the flow to avoid overwatering.

A watering can is ideal for a small garden setup but can be labor-intensive for larger gardens.

How to use it:

Pour water around the base of plants and avoid getting the foliage wet. For seedlings, use an attachment to disperse the stream or consider a gentler watering method to prevent disturbing their fragile roots.

Bottom Watering

Bottom watering involves allowing the soil to soak up water through the container's drainage holes rather than letting water soak down from the soil surface. This has its benefits as the water reaches the root zone much faster. It also saves water, as no surface evaporation occurs. Ensure your containers have drainage holes, or bottom watering won't work.

How to use the method:

1. Fill a shallow tray with water and put the container plant inside. Ensure the bottom of the container is entirely underwater so the soil can soak the water up.
2. Let the soil absorb water for a few hours.
3. Take the container out of the water and allow it to drip dry before putting it back in its spot.

Some specialized pots have a reservoir below the plant pot with a synthetic fiber connecting the two, allowing the plant to self-regulate its watering.

Gradual Flow Method

Plants can benefit from a slow and steady water supply in hot and dry weather. Some plants need constant soil moisture and will most benefit from maintaining consistent moisture levels. This method also has the benefit of being water-wise.

How to use:

- Install a drip irrigation system with emitters placed at the base of your plants or insert watering spikes into the soil near your plants, careful not to disturb the roots.
- Check the emitters daily for water levels, blockages, and even more regularly in hot weather.

You can make a simple device to water your plants gradually:

- Make a small hole 2–3 inches below the top of a plastic bottle.
- Fill the bottle with water and put the cap on.
- Turn it over and poke the bottle's neck into the ground, or support it with a stake.
- Check that the water can slowly drip from the bottle.

DRIP IRRIGATION

Drip irrigation is a water-efficient method that delivers a controlled, slow water drip directly to the base of plants through a network of tubes, pipes, valves, and emitters. This system ensures that water reaches the roots with minimal waste, making it a popular choice for gardens and landscapes.

While it has notable advantages, it's essential to weigh the pros and cons to determine if it aligns with your garden's specific requirements and your level of gardening experience.

Pros of Drip Irrigation

Water Efficiency

- Precise water application reduces water wastage.
- Targeted delivery to the root zone minimizes evaporation.

Conservation of Resources

- Reduces overall water consumption, promoting sustainability.
- Conserves time and energy compared to manual watering.

Healthy Plant Growth

- Provides a consistent water supply, promoting optimal plant health.
- Prevents foliage from getting wet, reducing the risk of fungal diseases.

Adaptability

- Suitable for various garden layouts, including raised beds, containers, and traditional soil beds.
- It can be automated with timers for convenient and consistent watering.

Weed Control

Directs water specifically to plants, minimizing weed growth in between.

Cons of Drip Irrigation

Initial Setup Complexity

- Requires proper planning and installation, which may be challenging for beginners.
- Initial costs for materials and setup can be higher.

Clogging Risk

- Emitter clogging may occur, affecting water distribution.
- Regular maintenance is necessary to prevent issues.

Dependency on Power

- Automated systems may rely on electricity, leading to interruptions during power outages.
- Battery-operated timers may need periodic replacement.

Not Suitable for All Plants

- Some plants may not benefit from drip irrigation as they prefer different watering methods.
- Requires careful consideration of plant types and their water needs.

Pros and Cons of Hand-Watering Plants

While hand-watering offers a personal touch and affordability, more extensive gardens require time and effort. You should weigh these pros and cons based on your preferences, garden size, and the specific needs of your plants.

Pros

- Allows for precise control over water placement, targeting the root zones of individual plants.
- Well-suited for gardens of various sizes, including small spaces and container gardens.
- Ideal for plants with diverse water requirements.
- Requires minimal initial investment in equipment.

- There is no need for complex irrigation systems or power sources.
- It provides the opportunity to visually inspect plants while watering them.
- Enables close monitoring of soil moisture and plant health.
- Watering frequency and amounts can be adjusted based on specific plant needs and weather conditions.
- Offers flexibility in response to changing environmental factors.

Cons

- It can be time-consuming, especially for more extensive gardens.
- Regular hand-watering may become physically demanding.
- Risk of uneven water distribution, leading to overwatering or underwatering.
- It relies on individual attention and may be affected by human error.
- Lack of automation requires a consistent personal schedule for watering.
- It is not suitable for those seeking hands-off or time-saving solutions.
- Runoff and water splatter can occur, resulting in water wastage.
- Less efficient than controlled systems in terms of water conservation.

- Weather conditions, such as wind or rain, can impact hand-watering effectiveness.
- Requires adjustment based on external factors.
- Some plants may be sensitive to overhead watering, increasing the risk of diseases.
- Certain soil types may not absorb water evenly with this method.

Dos and Don'ts of Hand-Watering Plants

The Dos

- Direct water to the base of the plants, focusing on the root zone to ensure adequate absorption.
- Watering in the morning allows plants to absorb moisture before the day's heat, reducing the risk of diseases.
- Employ tools like watering cans or hose nozzles with adjustable settings for better control and precision.
- Understand the water requirements of different plants in your garden and adjust watering frequency accordingly.
- Add enough water to moisten the soil, but not too much to cause waterlogging. Allow moisture to penetrate the root zone.
- Adapt your watering schedule based on weather conditions, considering factors like rain or increased temperatures.
- Regularly check soil moisture levels by inserting your finger into the soil up to the first knuckle. Water only if

the top inch or two of the soil is dry. Adjust watering based on the individual species' needs.

- Apply a layer of mulch around plants to retain soil moisture, reduce evaporation, and minimize weed growth.

The Don'ts

- Avoid excessive watering, leading to waterlogged soil, root rot, and other moisture-related issues.
- Refrain from watering during the hottest part of the day to minimize water loss through evaporation.
- Avoid high-pressure water streams that can damage soil and delicate plant structures.
- Pay extra attention to container plants, as they may dry out faster than those planted in the ground.
- Minimize overhead watering, especially in the evening, to prevent prolonged leaf wetness and reduce the risk of fungal diseases.
- Avoid watering stressed plants during extreme heat or cold, as they may not absorb water effectively.
- Recognize that watering needs to change with the seasons. Adjust your watering routine as temperatures and sunlight levels fluctuate.
- Be intentional and systematic in your watering approach, ensuring all plants receive adequate moisture.

HAND WATERING OR DRIP IRRIGATION

Drip irrigation and manual watering stand out as the two primary and recommended container watering methods. While manual watering aids in water conservation, it falls short in efficiency. In contrast, drip irrigation provides precise control over both watering duration and volume, ensuring conservation through tailored customization.

Consider your needs and your garden's needs when deciding which method will work best.

WATERING SCHEDULES AND TECHNIQUES FOR DIFFERENT PLANT TYPES

Watering schedules and techniques vary depending on the types of plants in your container garden. Understanding the specific needs of different plant types is crucial for maintaining optimal health and promoting vigorous growth.

Succulents and Cacti

You don't need to water these plants frequently, as they are well adapted to dry environments. The soil should be completely dry before watering. Provide a thorough soak, allowing water to reach the root zone. Ensure well-draining soil as their roots are sensitive to wet conditions.

Herbs

The soil must remain moist at all times. Water the base of the plants to avoid wetting the foliage. Consider drip irrigation or mulching to keep the soil moist.

Flowering Plants

Most flowering plants prefer even moisture. Test the soil with your finger, and water only once the top inch feels dry. Water at the base to avoid splashing water on flowers and foliage. Use a mulch layer to retain moisture and suppress weeds.

Vegetables

Vegetables often require consistent moisture, especially during fruiting. If the soil surface is dry, it's time to water. Water at the base to keep foliage dry and prevent disease. Drip irrigation or soaker hoses are beneficial for even moisture distribution.

Fruit Trees in Containers

Water deeply, but infrequently. Do the finger test and water if the top few inches of the soil is dry. You can add 2–4 inches of mulch to help preserve soil moisture. Adjust watering during fruit development.

Ferns and Tropical Plants

Maintain consistently moist soil. These plants typically thrive in higher humidity levels. Mist the foliage regularly to create a humid environment.

Grasses

Water grasses when the soil surface feels dry, but they can tolerate short periods of drought. Water deeply to encourage deep root growth. Consider aerating the soil to improve water penetration.

Shrubs in Containers

Water when the top two inches of soil is dry. Adjust the frequency based on the specific shrub's water requirements. Provide thorough watering to reach the entire root system— mulch to conserve soil moisture.

THE GOLDEN RULES OF WATERING PLANTS

Keep the following golden rules in mind when watering your plants; use them to create a checklist to refer to whenever you hydrate them:

1. Pre-water Before Planting

Always ensure the soil is adequately moist before planting or sowing seeds. Water the planting hole or seed drill if the soil is dry.

2. Optimal Watering Times

Water plants in the early morning or evening to minimize water evaporation, ensuring efficient water usage, especially when relying on municipal water.

3. Target the Base, Not the Leaves

Water plants around their base rather than wetting their leaves. This directs water to the root zone where the plant needs it the most.

4. Thoroughly Water Potted Plants

For potted or containerized plants and hanging baskets, continue watering until water flows through the bottom of the pot. This ensures they are thoroughly moistened.

5. Watering Frequency

Adjust the frequency of watering based on the specific needs of each plant. Consider soil type, weather conditions, and plant species to determine an appropriate watering schedule.

6. Soak, Don't Sprinkle

Opt for deep watering to encourage the development of a robust root system. A thorough soaking encourages roots to grow deeper into the soil.

7. Mulch for Moisture Retention

Add 2–4 inches of mulch to the container to preserve moisture. Mulching reduces evaporation, regulates soil temperature, and minimizes weed growth.

8. Check Soil Moisture Before Watering

Before watering, assess the soil moisture level. Stick your finger an inch or two into the soil to determine if watering is necessary. Moist, but not soggy, is the correct balance. Too much water can lead to poor plant health and even death.

9. Use a Watering Can or Drip System

Employ watering cans or drip irrigation systems for more controlled and targeted water application. This reduces water wastage and ensures efficient coverage.

10. Be Mindful of Plant Species

Different plants have varied water requirements. Familiarize yourself with the specific needs of each plant species in your garden.

11. Consider Microclimates

Recognize microclimates within your garden, accounting for variations in sunlight, wind exposure, and soil moisture. Adjust your watering approach accordingly.

12. Monitor Seasonal Changes

Adapt your watering routine to seasonal changes. Plants may require more water during hot and dry periods and less during cooler seasons.

13. Collect Rainwater

Take advantage of natural resources by collecting rainwater. Use rain barrels to harvest rainwater for watering your plants.

14. Regularly Inspect for Signs of Overwatering or Underwatering

Keep a close eye on your plants for signs of overwatering (yellowing leaves, root rot) or underwatering (wilting, dry soil). Adjust your watering practices accordingly.

IN SUMMARY

1. Different species of plants have varying light, temperature, and water requirements.
2. Observe the angle the sunlight comes from as well as how its position in the sky at different times of the day influences the exposure your plants receive.
3. Plants need a temperature range between 50–70°F. Extreme temperatures outside this range can harm your plants.
4. Water your plants properly by keeping the soil moist but not wet.
5. Use a watering can or drip irrigation to simplify watering.
6. Regularly check soil moisture levels by inserting your finger into the soil.
7. Regularly empty drip trays.
8. Use bottom watering to avoid disturbing newly planted seeds, seedlings, and fragile plants.
9. Use mulching to conserve moisture and insulate your plants' roots against extreme temperature fluctuations.

IN THE NEXT CHAPTER

Just like us, plants have their specific requirements to keep healthy and grow vigorously. Always make sure to read up on individual plants' to make sure they are getting everything they need to thrive. Next, we will be looking at how to prevent pest infestations, which garden pests are most common, and organic treatments to manage pests.

7

PEST MANAGEMENT TECHNIQUES

" *What is commonly called a pest is nature's way of bringing back into balance an imbalance that man has created.*

— ALAN CHADWICK

PEST PREVENTION

P revention stands as the most accessible and effective approach to organic garden pest control. By prioritizing preventive measures, you can reduce the likelihood of pest infestations and minimize the need for intervention later.

Here are various strategies and practices to safeguard your container garden from pests:

- Start with thoughtful garden planning, incorporating companion planting strategies that naturally deter pests.
- Choose pest-resistant plant varieties.
- Maintain overall garden health through proper watering, nutrient balance, and soil management, creating resilient plants and an inhospitable environment for pests.
- Regularly inspect plants for early signs of pest activity to allow for timely action and prevent issues from escalating.
- Attract beneficial insects, such as ladybugs, lacewings, and predatory beetles, as an environmentally friendly pest control option.
- Birds and spiders are natural predators that can contribute to pest management. Encourage their presence around your container garden.
- Use physical barriers like row covers or netting to protect plants from flying insects and pests.
- Place copper tape around containers to deter slugs and snails.
- Water your plants in the morning to allow the soil surface to dry during the day, reducing the risk of fungal diseases. Avoid overwatering, as damp conditions can attract pests.
- Regularly remove debris, fallen leaves, and dead plants from your container garden. Pests often hide in decaying matter. This practice reduces hiding spots and disrupts pest life cycles.

- Clean gardening tools regularly to prevent the spread of diseases between plants.

PESTICIDES

Pesticides are substances used to control or eliminate the pests that harm your plants. They are made of a variety of chemicals designed to repel, kill, or mitigate the impact of pests.

Natural pesticides are derived from naturally occurring substances, including minerals, plants, or microorganisms.

Organic pesticides, on the other hand, are specifically approved for use in organic farming, adhering to stringent guidelines that prioritize environmental sustainability.

Effective natural and organic pest control products include:

- Neem oil disrupts insect feeding and acts as a growth regulator.
- Diatomaceous earth, derived from fossilized algae, is an abrasive powder that damages the exoskeletons of insects.
- Insecticidal soaps and horticultural oils, such as neem or peppermint oil-based solutions, can effectively control pests without harming beneficial insects. These options provide environmentally friendly alternatives for pest management in gardens.

IDENTIFYING COMMON PESTS AND HOW TO TREAT YOUR PLANTS

Utilizing the following organic methods helps control common garden pests effectively while maintaining a balance in the garden ecosystem. It is still important to remember that pesticides—organic or not—do not discern between pests and beneficial insects, so take care to apply these treatments to the pest insects only.

Aphids

Aphids are small, soft-bodied insects that feed on plant sap, often found in clusters on the undersides of leaves.

Organic treatments:

- **Neem oil:** Neem oil disrupts aphids' feeding and reproductive cycles. Spray a neem oil solution on affected plants.
- **Insecticidal soap:** Mix insecticidal soap with water and spray it directly on aphids. The soap disrupts their cell membranes.
- **Beneficial insects:** Attract aphids' natural predators, like ladybugs, lacewings, or parasitic wasps, or purchase ladybugs online to solve your aphid problem.
- **Garlic spray:** Blend garlic cloves with water and allow to stand overnight, then strain out the solids and spray the garlic water on plants. Aphids find the scent repulsive.

Slugs

Slugs are soft-bodied, slimy pests that chew irregular holes in leaves and can damage seedlings.

Organic treatments:

- **Beer traps:** Bury containers filled with beer in the soil. Slugs are attracted to the beer, fall in, and drown.

- **Copper barriers:** Place copper tape or barriers around containers. Slugs get a mild electric shock when they touch it, deterring them.
- **Diatomaceous earth:** Sprinkle food-grade diatomaceous earth around plants. It dehydrates and kills slugs.
- **Handpicking**: Go out at night—when slugs are active— and handpick them off plants. Dispose of them away from the garden.

Tomato Hornworms

Big, green caterpillars that feed on blossoms, leaves, and fruit. Organic treatments:

- **Handpicking**: Simply pick hornworms off by hand and drop them into a bucket of soapy water.
- **Beneficial insects**: Encourage natural predators like parasitic wasps and braconid wasps, which lay eggs on hornworms.
- **Bt (*Bacillus thuringiensis*)**: Bt is a naturally occurring bacterium that is toxic to many caterpillar pests. Apply it as a spray.

Whiteflies

Tiny, white, moth-like insects that cluster on the undersides of leaves, sucking plant sap.

Organic treatments:

- **Yellow sticky traps:** Hang yellow sticky traps near affected plants. Whiteflies are attracted to the color and get stuck.
- **Neem oil:** Neem oil disrupts the life cycle of whiteflies. Spray a neem oil solution on plants.
- **Insecticidal soap:** Use insecticidal soap to coat whiteflies and kill them. Ensure thorough coverage on the undersides of leaves.

Snails

Snails have a hard shell and leave slime trails. They can eat large portions of leaves, stems, and fruits.

Organic treatments:

- **Beer traps:** Similar to slugs, snails are attracted to beer. Bury containers filled with beer in the soil.
- **Copper barriers:** Use copper tape or barriers around planters to create an electric shock deterrent.
- **Crushed eggshells:** Create a barrier of crushed eggshells around plants. Snails avoid crawling over sharp edges.

Cabbage Worms

The larvae of white butterflies and cabbage worms are green caterpillars that feed on cabbage, broccoli, and other brassicas.

Organic treatments:

- **Floating row covers:** Use lightweight fabric covers to block adult butterflies from laying eggs on plants physically.
- **Bt**: Apply Bt as a spray. It's safe for humans but deadly for cabbage worms.
- **Handpicking**: Regularly inspect plants and pick off caterpillars. Dispose of them away from the garden.

Leaf Miner

Leaf miners are larvae that tunnel through leaves, creating distinctive patterns. Organic treatments:

- **Beneficial insects:** Encourage parasitic wasps, predatory beetles, and other beneficial insects that prey on leaf miners.
- **Neem oil**: Apply neem oil as a foliar spray. It disrupts the life cycle of leaf miners.
- **Remove infested leaves:** Prune and remove leaves with visible tunnels to reduce the population.

TIPS FOR PEST MANAGEMENT AND PREVENTION

Effective pest management in container gardens begins with proactive and regular monitoring. By staying vigilant, you can detect potential issues early, preventing widespread infestations and minimizing the need for intensive interventions. Here's a more detailed exploration:

- Ensure your container garden has nutrient-rich, well-draining soil for healthy, pest-resilient plants. Use compost to enrich the soil with beneficial microorganisms.
- Provide proper care, including adequate watering and fertilization. Healthy plants are less susceptible to pest infestations. Monitor for signs of stress or disease and address them promptly.
- Begin with non-invasive methods like handpicking pests or using water sprays. Introduce natural predators and consider companion planting. Patience allows the garden's natural balance to take effect.
- If a plant is heavily infested and efforts to control pests prove challenging, consider removing the affected plant to prevent the infestation from spreading. This can protect the overall health of your container garden.
- Establish a routine for inspecting your container garden. Check both the upper and lower surfaces of leaves, stems, and the soil around plants. Look for signs of pest activity, including chewed leaves, discoloration, or the presence of pests themselves.

- Be familiar with common pests that can affect container plants. Aphids, caterpillars, spider mites, and scale insects are among the usual suspects. Identifying pests accurately is crucial for choosing appropriate control methods.
- If you identify a heavily infested plant, consider isolating it temporarily to prevent the pests from spreading. In some cases, removing severely affected plants might be necessary to safeguard the health of the entire container garden.
- Homemade or commercially available insecticidal soaps can be effective against soft-bodied pests like aphids and spider mites. These solutions work by disrupting the outer cell membranes of insects, causing them to dehydrate.
- Pest dynamics can change over time, influenced by factors like weather and plant growth stages. Regularly observe your container garden, especially during vulnerable periods like new growth or flowering, and adjust your pest management strategies accordingly.

IN SUMMARY

- Emphasize preventive measures for effective organic pest control, reducing the need for intervention later.
- Incorporate companion planting strategies for natural pest deterrence during thoughtful garden planning.
- Opt for pest-resistant plant varieties to fortify your container garden against potential infestations.

- Ensure overall garden health through proper watering, nutrient balance, and soil management, creating resilient plants and an inhospitable environment for pests.
- Regularly inspect plants for early signs of pest activity, facilitating timely action to prevent issues from escalating.
- Attract ladybugs, lacewings, predatory beetles, birds, and spiders as natural predators to manage pests eco-friendly.
- Use row covers, netting, and copper tape to create physical barriers, protecting plants from flying insects, slugs, and snails.
- Consider natural and organic pesticides like neem oil, diatomaceous earth, insecticidal soaps, and horticultural oils for environmentally friendly pest management.
- Utilize specific organic treatments for each pest, including neem oil, insecticidal soap, beneficial insects, beer traps, copper barriers, diatomaceous earth, Bt, and more.
- Begin with non-invasive methods, like handpicking and natural predators, before resorting to more intensive interventions.
- Establish a routine for inspecting the container garden checking leaves, stems, and soil for signs of pests.
- Regularly observe the container garden, adjusting pest management strategies based on changing dynamics influenced by weather and plant growth stages.

IN THE NEXT CHAPTER

Now that you know what to look out for and how to prevent
and treat pest infestations in the garden, you can go ahead and
make informed decisions when choosing pest- resilient plants
for your containers. Next, we'll be looking at how to grow
vegetables, berries, fruit and herbs in containers, as well as a
few mouthwatering recipes you can make with your crops.

8

GROWING YOUR OWN FOOD

A person who is growing a garden, if he is growing it organically, is improving a piece of the world. He is producing something to eat, which makes him somewhat independent of the grocery business, but he is also enlarging, for himself, the meaning of food and the pleasure of eating.

— WENDELL BERRY

GROWING FRESH VEGETABLES AND HERBS

Recommended Varieties

The varieties in the table below were chosen for their yield, ease of growing, and overall performance.

Vegetables	Container Size	Recommended Varieties	When To Plant	Notes and Tips
Asian Greens	Depth: least 4–8 inches	At Bok Choy, Mizuna, Chinese Mustard Greens, Green Amaranth, Tatsoi	Mid-March to May	These greens grow fast and have shallow roots. When grown as baby greens, they require as little as 4 inches of soil.
Basil	Depth: At least 8 inches	Dark Genovese, Opal, Globe, Largeleaf Italian, Osmin Purple, Purple Ruffles, Red Rubin, Siam Queen,	June to August	Plant basil as a companion to tomatoes to improve their flavor.
		Spicy Globe, Sweet Basil		At 6–8 inches, pinch off the growing tip to encourage branching.
Green Beans	Size: 10–12 inches in diameter Depth: At least 6 inches	Tricolor bush and pole varieties, Blue Lake, Romano, Jade, Fortex, Kentucky Wonder	June to August	Pole varieties are great for vertical gardening or creating shade. Plant as a companion to brassicas like Bok choy, cabbage, and broccoli to benefit from the beans' nitrogen-fixing ability.

Beets	Size: 10–12 inches in diameter Depth: At least 10 inches deep	Detroit Dark Red, Avalanch, Chioggia, Merlin, Early Wonder, Moulin Rouge	Mid-March to May	Beets are hardy and can grow in partial sun. Harvest beets at around golf ball size before they become tough and woody. The greens are also edible.
Broccoli	Volume: One plant per 5-gallon container	De Ciccom, Purple Sprouting Broccoli, Romanesco, Waltham	Mid-March to May	Early maturing, compact varieties are easier to grow.
Brussels Sprouts	Volume: One plant per 5-gallon container	Churchill, Catskill, Mighty, Nelson, Tasty Nuggets, Long Island Improved, Diablo	Plant in March for a late fall harvest.	Brussels sprouts take 80–90 days to reach harvestable sizes.
Cabbage	Volume: One plant per 5-gallon container	Farao, Typhoon, Tiara, Tropic Giant, Charleston Wakefield, Savoy, Red Cabbage, Alcosa	Plant in March for a mid-summer harvest.	Harvest lettuce heads by cutting only the head off and leaving the outer leaves to continue growing. This increases the chance of a second harvest of multiple smaller heads.
Carrot	Depth: At least 8 inches deep	Purple Dragon, Thumbelina, Tendersweet, Salar Yellow, Lunar White, Imperator 58	February to April and August to October	Carrots can be harvested at any size, but smaller carrots are more tender. The entire plant is edible; the greens are great in salads.

Swiss Chard	Depth: At least 8 inches deep	Fordhook Giant, Charbell, Magic, Lucullus, Oriole, Bright Lights, Pink Lipstick, Perpetual Spinach	Red	Mid-March to May	Varieties like Fordhook Giant can grow indefinitely by harvesting the outer leaves regularly.
Collard Greens	Depth: At least 8 inches deep	Tiger Hybrid, Ellen Felten Dark, Old Timey Blue, Vates, Georgia, Champion, Groninger Blauw		Mid-March to May	Collard greens are tastier and more nutritious when they are grown in cool weather.
Cucumber	Volume: One plant per 3 to 5-gallon container	Ashley, Burpless #26, Dasher II, Diva, Fanfare, Marketer, Straight Eight, Tanja, Fancipak		June to August	Comes in bush and vining varieties. Opt for vining varieties to grow them vertically.
Eggplant	Volume: One plant per 3- gallon container	Black Beauty, Clara, Pinstripe, Turkish Orange, Rosa Bianca, Bonica, Purple Graffiti		June to August	Provide a trellis to support the plant when producing heavy fruits.
Garlic	Depth: At least 8 inches deep	Spanish Roja, Stu:, Reisig, Pennsylvania Dutch, Red Rezen, Music, Krasnador Red, German Red		October for harvesting the following July	Pre-soak garlic cloves in alcohol for 20 minutes to sterilize them, then soak them for a day in diluted fish emulsion to pre-fertilize the cloves.

Green Onion	Depth: At least 8 inches deep or shallower for smaller plants	Crystal Wax, Tokyo Long, White Portugal, Eclipse, Kincho, Ishikura, Hishiko, Ebenezer	Mid-March to October	Green onions are fast-growing and much easier to cultivate than onions.
Kale	Depth: At least 8 inches deep	Lacinato, Red Russian, Chinese Kale, Redbor, Siberian, Common Curly Kale	Mid-March to May	Kale is extremely frost-resistant and can even tolerate snow. They will, however, grow far slower in winter.
Lettuce	Depth: At least 4 inches deep	Crisphead: Igloo, Hanson Improved, Crisphead Great Lakes. Butterhead: Dynamite, Four Seasons, Tom Thumb. Romaine: Vivian, Cimarron, Little Caesar. Loose Leaf: Deer Tongue, Ruby, Lollo Rosso	Mid-March to October	Loose-leaf varieties can be harvested as you need them. Baby lettuce can be grown in very shallow containers.
Parsley	Depth: At least 8 inches deep	Aphrodite, Green Pearl, Curly Moss, Riccio Verde, Mitsuba Bronze and Purpurascens	Mid-March to May	Parsley germinates very slowly, taking up to six weeks.
Peas	Depth: 6–8 inches deep	Avola, Canoe, Capucinjer, Cascadia, Tendersweet, Sugar Daddy	Mid-March to May	Provide a trellis to support peas. Harvest snap peas early in the morning for the best flavor.
Peppers	Volume: One plant per 2-gallon container	Bell peppers, Jalapeño, Sessano, Poblano, Cherry Pepper	June to August	Peppers love warm temperatures up to 90°F.

Potatoes	Size: 18 inches in diameter	Red Gold, Rio Grande, Magic Molly. Masquerade. Yukon Gold, Kennebec	June to August	Potatoes are grown from seed potatoes with buds.
	Depth: Start with 10 inches of soil in a 36-			Hill the soil up around the plant
	inch deep container			to 6 inches high when the plants are about 10 inches tall.
Radish	Depth: At least 4–6 inches deep	Daikon, German Giant, Red King, Early Scarlet Globe, Cherry Belle, Hailstone, Golden Helios	Mid-March to May	Radish grows quickly, taking only four weeks from seed to table. Avoid using nitrogen-rich fertilizers.
Spinach	Depth: At least 8 inches deep	Acadia, Auroch, Butterflay, Carmel, Emperor, Flamingo, Gazelle, Persius	Mid-March to May	Plant in early spring and again in fall; spinach does not tolerate heat well and will bolt in warm temperatures.
Summer Squash	Volume: One plant per 5- gallon container	Supersett, Zephyr, Caserta, Cocozelle, Rheinau Gold, Tatume, Sunburst	June to August	A female flower has a tiny fruit at its base. Collect pollen from the male flowers using a Q-tip or a small brush and deposit it inside the female flowers to aid in pollination.
Tomatoes	Volume: One plant per 5- gallon container	Striped German, Brandywine, Black Beauty, Midnight Roma, Juliet, Sunrise Bumblebee	June to August	Prune tomato suckers—new stems that sprout at the base of larger branches— to divert more of the plant's energy to producing fruit.

HOW TO GROW, MAINTAIN, AND TAKE CARE OF VEGETABLES IN A CONTAINER GARDEN

Growing fresh vegetables and herbs is a rewarding activity that makes the vibrant essence of a garden part of your daily life. Cultivating your own vegetables and herbs allows you to savor the unparalleled freshness and flavors of homegrown produce. From the joy of seeing seeds sprout to the satisfaction of harvesting your first ripe tomatoes or fragrant basil leaves, each step in the gardening process is a celebration of nature's abundance.

Creating a flourishing container garden for fresh vegetables is easy and fun, even for beginners. Follow these easy tips to grow, maintain, and care for vegetables in your container garden and to ensure its success:

Sunlight

- Sunlight intensity varies throughout the day as the sun moves across the sky. Morning sunlight is gentler, making it suitable for plants that prefer softer light. Afternoon sun is more intense and benefits plants that thrive in higher light levels. Consider these patterns when placing your containers, ensuring that each vegetable gets the light it needs.
- Different vegetables have varying sunlight preferences. Some, like cucumbers and peppers, are considered full-sun plants, requiring at least 6 hours of direct sunlight.

Others, such as lettuce and certain herbs, are partial-sun or shade- tolerant, thriving with 3 to 6 hours of bright light. Match the sunlight requirements of your chosen vegetables with the conditions in your garden.

- Proper sunlight exposure directly impacts the growth, flowering, and fruiting of vegetables. Placing containers in sunny spots promotes robust growth, leading to better yields and healthier plants.
- Sunlight patterns shift with the changing seasons due to Earth's orbit around the sun. Understanding these variations is essential for planning a container garden for year-round success. Be mindful of how sunlight exposure changes during different seasons and adjust your container placement accordingly.

Water

- Maintaining consistent moisture in the soil is essential for the health of your container plants. While each plant has specific water requirements, a general guideline is to keep the soil consistently moist.
- Some plants, like herbs and succulents, prefer drier conditions, while others, such as leafy greens and tomatoes, need more frequent watering. Be aware of the specific needs of each plant in your garden and adjust your watering routine accordingly.
- Consistent and appropriate watering prevents water stress in plants. Water stress can lead to issues such as wilting, reduced fruiting, and increased susceptibility to pests and diseases.

Soil

- Good drainage is essential to prevent waterlogging. Ensure the potting mix has a mix of materials like perlite, vermiculite, or sand to promote drainage. Avoid using garden soil, as it tends to compact in containers, hindering drainage and aeration.
- Enhance soil fertility by regularly incorporating organic matter into the potting mix. Compost, well-rotted manure, or other organic amendments contribute valuable nutrients, improve water retention, and promote beneficial microbial activity in the soil.
- Container plants rely on the nutrients present in the potting mix, as they can't draw from the surrounding soil. Choose a mix with a balanced blend of essential nutrients or supplement with a slow-release fertilizer to provide a steady nutrient supply throughout the growing season.
- Check the pH level of the potting mix to ensure it falls within the appropriate range for the plants you intend to grow. Most plants prefer a soil pH of 6.0 to 7.0, slightly more on the acidic side. Adjustments can be made to the pH with additives like lime to make the soil more acidic and sulfur to make it more basic.
- Depending on the specific needs of your plants, consider soil amendments. For example, to improve drainage and aeration and to loosen clay structures, amend soil with gypsum.
- Consider applying a layer of organic mulch on the soil surface. Mulch helps regulate soil temperature, reduce

evaporation, and suppress weed growth. Organic mulches like straw or bark also break down over time, adding organic matter to the soil. Inorganic mulches you can also consider are landscaping fabric and pebbles or stones.

- Tailor your choice of vegetables to the type of potting mix you use. Some vegetables and herbs do well in a general-purpose mix, while others, like cucumbers or summer squash, benefit from a soil mix with added compost or fertilizers.

Fertilizing

- Container plants rely on the nutrients available in the potting mix, and over time, these nutrients can become depleted. Fertilizing ensures that your plants receive a balanced supply of essential elements, promoting robust growth, vibrant foliage, and abundant blooms or fruit.
- Opt for a water-soluble fertilizer suitable for container gardening. This type of fertilizer dissolves in water, making it easy to apply and quickly available to the plant roots. It's essential to choose a fertilizer with a balanced NPK to meet the overall nutritional needs of your plants.
- Follow the package instructions for the specific fertilizer you're using. Generally, container plants benefit from regular feeding during the growing season, which is when they are actively producing new leaves, flowers, or fruit. This often means fertilizing every two

to four weeks, but the frequency can vary based on the fertilizer formulation and the plants you're growing.

- Excessive fertilizer can lead to the buildup of salts in the soil, causing root damage and negatively impacting plant health. Always follow the recommended application rates on the fertilizer package to prevent overfeeding.
- Apply fertilizer when the soil is moist to facilitate nutrient absorption by the roots. Water the plants before applying fertilizer, and avoid fertilizing plants that are already stressed due to factors like extreme temperatures or insufficient water.
- Different plants may have varying nutrient requirements. Some plants, like leafy greens, may benefit from higher nitrogen levels for lush foliage, while flowering plants may need more phosphorus to support blooming. Be aware of the specific needs of the plants in your container garden and choose a fertilizer formulation that aligns with those needs.
- For a more hands-off approach, consider using slow-release fertilizers. These granular fertilizers release nutrients gradually over an extended period, providing a steady supply to the plants. This can be particularly convenient for busy gardeners.

Companion Planting

Companion planting is a strategic gardening method that involves growing mutually beneficial plants in close proximity. This practice is particularly valuable in container gardens, where space optimization and pest control are essential. Embracing companion planting in your container garden not only enhances the aesthetic appeal of your space but also creates a naturally resilient and thriving ecosystem that reduces the reliance on chemical interventions while fostering plant health and productivity.

Here's a more detailed exploration of companion planting:

- Companion planting relies on the principle that growing certain plants together enhances each other's growth, repels pests, or improves soil conditions. In container gardens, these relationships are used to create a harmonious and pest-resistant environment.
- One classic example is planting basil alongside tomatoes. Basil emits aromatic compounds that naturally repel common tomato pests like aphids. This not only protects tomatoes from potential damage but also provides a flavor-enhancing partnership as these herbs are often used together in culinary applications.
- Explore other companion planting combinations suitable for containers. Marigolds, for instance, release substances that deter nematodes and other soil- borne pests. Nasturtiums can act as a trap crop, luring aphids away from more susceptible plants.
- Companion planting reduces the need for chemical pesticides, promoting a more natural and environmentally friendly approach to pest management. By carefully selecting plant companions, you create a living ecosystem that minimizes the

presence of harmful insects while fostering a healthy balance between pests and their natural predators.

- Companion planting allows you to make the most of every inch. Pairing plants with complementary growth habits ensures efficient use of space, preventing overcrowding and promoting optimal growth conditions.
- Before planting, research the compatibility and mutual benefits of different vegetables, herbs, and flowers. Consider factors such as sunlight requirements, water needs, and growth habits to create a well-balanced garden.
- Companion planting is flexible and can be adapted to the constraints of container gardening. For example, if growing space is limited, consider planting vertically using trellises or tiered containers to maximize the benefits of companion plants.
- Regularly observe your container garden to identify any signs of pest infestations or poor growth. Adjust your companion planting arrangements as needed, and be open to experimenting with new combinations based on your observations and experiences.

Crop Rotation

Crop rotation is a proactive approach to cultivating healthier plants and ecosystems. Crop rotation involves changing the types of crops you grow in specific areas or pots over successive seasons. This strategic rotation offers various benefits for both soil health and pest management:

- Different crops have distinct nutrient needs and contributions to the soil. Crop rotation helps maintain a balanced nutrient profile in the soil, preventing the depletion of specific elements.
- Certain plants release compounds that suppress soil-borne diseases. By rotating crops, the buildup of diseases affecting specific plant types is minimized.
- Pests and diseases often have specific host plants. Rotating crops disrupts the life cycles of pests, reducing their prevalence in the soil and preventing infestations.
- Beneficial insects are natural predators that prey on pests. They may establish themselves when a different crop is introduced. This balance helps naturally control pest populations and reduces the reliance on chemical pesticides, promoting sustainable and eco-friendly farming practices.
- Crop rotation can interfere with the life cycles of certain weeds. For example, growing crops with dense canopies may suppress weed growth, offering a natural form of weed control.
- Different crops have varied root structures. Crop rotation enhances root diversity in the soil, contributing to improved soil structure, aeration, and water retention.
- Plants within the same botanical family, like potato and tomato—nightshades— and Swiss chard and beetroot—the beet family, or amaranthaceae— often share pests and diseases. Crop rotation involves changing the plant family in a specific location, reducing the risk of persistent family-specific issues.

Plant Selection

If you're new to container gardening, start with vegetables that are known for their adaptability and relatively straightforward care.

Cucumbers, peppers, loose-leaf lettuce, and various herbs are excellent choices for beginners. These plants are generally more forgiving and less demanding in terms of maintenance.

Herbs are well-suited for containers, and they can be grown individually or combined in a herb garden. Popular herbs like rosemary, mint, basil, and sage are not only culinary delights but also add fragrance and aesthetic appeal to your container garden.

FRUIT TREES AND BERRIES IN CONTAINERS

Growing berries and fruit trees in container gardens offer you fresh, flavorful fruits right at your fingertips. Pay attention to the specific needs of each plant, including their soil, sunlight, and pruning requirements. With proper care, you can enjoy a fruitful harvest from your compact garden. To ensure success, consider the following tips and guidance:

Hardiness

- Select berry varieties that thrive in your local climate and are well-suited for container cultivation.

- Verify the hardiness zones of the chosen berries to ensure they can withstand the winter temperatures in your region.

Space and Plant Size Considerations

- Opt for large containers to provide ample space for root growth. Fruit trees and berries, especially those with spreading habits, benefit from roomy containers.
- Opt for compact or dwarf varieties, as they are better suited to the limited space of containers. These plants are often more manageable in terms of size, making them ideal for smaller settings like balconies or patios.

Location and Light Exposure

- Berries and fruit trees typically require full sun for optimal fruiting. Place containers in locations that receive at least 6–8 hours of direct sunlight daily. Rotate the pots occasionally to expose all sides of the plant to sunlight evenly.
- Shield containers from strong winds, especially during fruiting, to prevent damage to delicate branches.

Personal Preferences

Consider your taste preferences when selecting fruit and berry varieties. Whether it's sweet figs, tart raspberries, or juicy blueberries, choose what you love, and you will be more invested in their care.

General Care

- Larger containers provide better insulation against temperature fluctuations and offer more room for root growth.
- Use a good nutrient-rich potting mix with adequate drainage. Ensure the mix is suitable for acid-loving berries like blueberries.
- Periodically re-pot plants to refresh the soil and provide additional space for growth.
- Berries prefer slightly acidic soil conditions, so use rainwater or add soil amendments when watering if possible.
- Regularly prune to remove dead or diseased wood and encourage new growth. Pruning also helps maintain the shape of the plant.
- During the growing season, use a slow-release fertilizer with a balanced NPK ratio. Follow package instructions for application rates.
- Monitor for pests regularly. Use natural remedies or organic insecticides to protect your plants without using harmful chemicals.

Recommended Fruits and Berries

Highbush Blueberry

- **Container size:** Choose a large container with acidic soil to mimic their preferred conditions.

- **Sunlight**: Full sun exposure is crucial for optimal fruiting.

- **Care tips**: Regular pruning and acidic fertilizer enhance growth.

Raspberry

- **Container size:** Opt for a large container to accommodate their spreading nature.
- **Support**: Install stakes or a trellis to support taller plants.
- **Sunlight**: Full sun to partial shade is ideal for raspberries.

Strawberry

- **Container size:** Hanging baskets or strawberry pots work well.
- **Soil**: Well-draining soil rich in organic matter.
- **Sunlight**: Full sun is essential for sweet, juicy berries.

Blackberries

- **Container size:** Large containers with a support system.
- **Support**: A trellis or stakes for the sprawling vines.
- **Care tips:** Prune regularly to manage growth and encourage fruiting.

Common Fig

- **Container size:** Medium-sized containers with well-draining soil.
- **Sunlight**: Full sun is essential.
- **Pruning**: Prune to control size and encourage fruiting.

Pineapple

- **Container size:** Use a large, deep container to accommodate the pineapple's root system.
- **Growing tips**: Plant the pineapple crown in well-draining soil. It requires bright sunlight and can be moved indoors during colder seasons.

Cantaloupe

- **Container size:** Choose a large container that has good drainage.
- **Growing tips:** Cantaloupes thrive in warm climates. Ensure the container receives ample sunlight and provides support for the vines as they grow.

Gooseberries

- **Container size:** Use a medium-sized container with well-draining soil.
- **Growing tips:** Gooseberries are well-suited for containers. They prefer cooler climates, so provide

partial shade in warmer regions. Prune to maintain shape and encourage airflow.

Mulberries

- **Container size:** Opt for a large container.
- **Growing tips:** Mulberries are adaptable to containers. Choose a dwarf or weeping variety for a more compact size. Provide well-draining soil and ample sunlight.

Passion Fruit

- **Container size:** Use a large container with a trellis or support for climbing vines.
- **Growing tips:** Passion fruit vines thrive in containers. They require well-draining soil, full sunlight, and a sturdy support structure. Regular pruning promotes fruit production.

General Tips for Growing Fruits in Containers

- Ensure containers have proper drainage to prevent waterlogging.
- Use a high-quality potting mix enriched with organic matter for nutrient retention.
- Consider how large you want the tree to get and choose suitably large containers.
- Provide adequate support for climbing or vining fruits.
- Monitor water and nutrient requirements, adjusting based on specific fruit varieties.

CULINARY DELIGHTS WITH YOUR HOMEGROWN PRODUCE

After growing your bumper crop comes the important question: How to prepare your harvest? Here are a few mouthwatering recipes you can try out:

Easy Stuffed Poblano Peppers

Preparation time: 25 minutes Servings: 4

Ingredients:

- 1/2 pound of Italian turkey sausage links, with casings removed
- 1/2 pound of 90% lean ground beef
- 1 package—8.8 ounces—of Spanish rice, ready-to-serve
- 4 large poblano peppers
- 1 cup of enchilada sauce
- 1/2 cup of shredded Mexican cheese blend
- Optional: Minced fresh cilantro

Instructions:

1. Begin by preheating the broiler. In a large skillet, cook the turkey and beef over medium heat until they are no longer pink, typically 5–7 minutes. Break the meat into crumbles and drain any excess fat.
2. Follow the package directions to prepare the Spanish rice. Combine the cooked rice with the meat mixture.
3. Cut the poblano peppers lengthwise in half and remove the seeds. Place them on a foil-lined baking pan with the cut side facing down. Broil them 4 inches from the heat source until the skins blister, which usually takes about 5 minutes. Use tongs to turn the peppers.

4. Fill each pepper halfway with the turkey and rice mixture. Top them with enchilada sauce and sprinkle the shredded Mexican cheese blend over them.

Broil until the cheese is melted, which typically takes 1–2 minutes. If desired, garnish with minced fresh cilantro.

Smoky Grilled Pizza with Greens & Tomatoes

Preparation time: 25 minutes Servings: 4

Ingredients for the base:

- 3 cups of all-purpose flour
- 2 teaspoons of kosher salt
- 1 teaspoon of active dry yeast
- 3 tablespoons of olive oil, divided
- 1-1/4 to 1-1/2 cups of warm water—120°F to 130°F
  Ingredients for the topping:
- 2 tablespoons of olive oil
- 10 cups of coarsely chopped beet greens
- 4 minced garlic cloves
- 2 tablespoons of balsamic vinegar
- 3/4 cup of prepared pesto
- 3/4 cup of shredded Italian cheese blend
- 1/2 cup of crumbled feta cheese
- 2 medium heirloom tomatoes, thinly sliced
- 1/4 cup of chopped fresh basil leaves

Directions:

1. In a food processor, combine flour, salt, and yeast; pulse until well blended. While processing, add 2 tablespoons of oil and enough water in a steady stream for the dough to form a ball. Transfer the dough onto a floured surface and knead until it becomes smooth and elastic approximately 6–8 minutes.
2. Place the kneaded dough in a greased bowl, turning it once to coat the top. Cover and let it rise in a warm place until it almost doubles in size, approximately 90 minutes.
3. Punch down the dough, then on a lightly floured surface, divide it into two portions. Press or roll each portion into a 10-inch circle and place them on greased foil. Brush the tops with the remaining oil, cover, and let them rest for 10 minutes.
4. For the topping, heat oil in a stockpot over medium-high heat. Add beet greens and cook until tender, stirring for 3–5 minutes. Add the minced garlic and cook for 30 more seconds. Remove from heat and stir in balsamic vinegar.
5. Carefully invert the pizza crusts onto the oiled grill rack, removing the foil. Grill covered over medium heat until the bottoms are lightly browned, which usually takes 3–5 minutes. Turn and grill until the second side begins to brown, about 1–2 minutes.
6. Remove the pizzas from the grill, spread them with pesto, and top with beet greens, cheeses, and tomatoes. Return the pizzas to the grill and cook covered over

medium heat until the cheese is melted, taking approximately 2–4 minutes. Finally, sprinkle with chopped basil before serving.

Crunchy Lemon-Pesto Garden Salad

Preparation time: 25 minutes Servings: 6

Dressing ingredients:

- 5 tablespoons of prepared pesto
- 1 tablespoon of lemon juice
- 2 teaspoons of grated lemon zest
- 1-1/2 teaspoons of Dijon mustard
- 1/4 teaspoon of garlic salt
- 1/4 teaspoon of pepper Salad ingredients:
- 2-1/2 cups of thinly sliced yellow summer squash
- 1-3/4 cups of thinly sliced mini cucumbers
- 3/4 cup of fresh peas
- 1/2 cup of shredded Parmesan cheese
- 1/4 cup of thinly sliced green onions
- 5 strips of thick-sliced bacon

Directions:

1. Cook the bacon until it's crispy. Let it cool on top of a sheet or two of paper towels to absorb the excess oil.
2. Whisk together the dressing ingredients in a bowl until they are well blended.

3. In another bowl, combine the sliced squash, cucumbers, peas, Parmesan cheese, and green onions.
4. Pour the dressing over the salad and toss the leaves to coat them evenly.
5. Top the salad with crumbled bacon, and serve.

Strawberry Kale Salad

Preparation time: 25 minutes Servings: 10

Dressing ingredients:

- 1/2 cup of olive oil
- 1/3 cup of cider vinegar
- 1 teaspoon of honey
- 1/4 teaspoon of salt
- 1/8 teaspoon of pepper Salad ingredients:
- 1 bunch of kale—approximately 12 ounces—trimmed and chopped
- 2 cups of sliced fresh strawberries
- 3/4 pound of cooked and crumbled bacon strips
- 1/4 cup of minced fresh mint
- 1 cup of crumbled feta cheese
- 1/4 cup of toasted slivered almonds

Directions:

1. Whisk together the ingredients for the dressing.
2. In a large bowl, combine the kale, strawberries, bacon, and mint. Toss the salad with the prepared dressing.

3. Sprinkle with feta cheese and toasted slivered almonds before serving.

Garden Vegetable Gnocchi

Preparation time: 30 minutes Servings: 4

Ingredients:

- 2 medium yellow summer squash, sliced
- 1 medium sweet red pepper, chopped
- 8 ounces of sliced fresh mushrooms
- 1 tablespoon of olive oil
- 1/4 teaspoon of salt
- 1/4 teaspoon of pepper
- 1 package—16 ounces—of potato gnocchi
- 1/2 cup of Alfredo sauce
- 1/4 cup of prepared pesto
- Chopped fresh basil

Directions:

1. Preheat the oven to 450°F. Toss the sliced vegetables with oil, salt, and pepper in a greased baking pan. Roast for 18—22 minutes or until the vegetables are tender, stirring once during the process.
2. Meanwhile, in a large saucepan, cook the gnocchi according to the package directions. Drain and return them to the pan.

3. Stir in the roasted vegetables, Alfredo sauce, and pesto into the saucepan with the gnocchi. If desired, sprinkle the dish with chopped fresh basil before serving.

Simple Grilled Steak Fajitas

Preparation time: 30 minutes Servings: 4

Ingredient:

- 1 pound of beef top sirloin steak, about 3/4 of an inch thick.
- 2 tablespoons of fajita seasoning mix
- 1 large sweet onion, sliced crosswise into 1/2-inch pieces
- 1 medium sweet red pepper cut in half
- 1 medium green pepper cut in half
- 1 tablespoon of olive oil
- 4 large whole wheat tortillas
- Optional toppings: Sliced avocado, minced fresh cilantro, and lime wedges

Directions:

1. Rub the steak with the fajita seasoning mix. Brush the onion and peppers with olive oil.
2. Grill the steak and vegetables, covered, on a greased rack over medium direct heat for 4–6 minutes on each side. Cook until the vegetables become tender and the meat reaches the desired doneness. For medium-rare, a

thermometer should read 135°F; medium, 140°F; and medium-well, 145°F.

3. Remove from the grill. Allow the steak to stand, covered, for 5 minutes before slicing.
4. Warm up the tortillas.
5. Cut the vegetables and steak into strips and serve them in the tortillas. If desired, top with sliced avocado and cilantro and serve with lime wedges.

IN SUMMARY

- Choose vegetable varieties for container gardening based on yield, ease of growing, and overall performance.
- Consider the morning sun for gentler light and the afternoon sun for higher intensity, placing containers accordingly.
- Keep soil consistently moist, adjusting based on plant-specific water needs.
- Prioritize proper drainage, organic matter, balanced nutrient supply, and pH levels in the potting mix.
- Use water-soluble fertilizers with a balanced NPK ratio, avoiding over-fertilization.
- Utilize companion planting to enhance growth, repel pests, and optimize space in container gardens.
- Implement crop rotation to promote soil health, manage pests, and support diverse root structures.
- Start with beginner-friendly vegetables like cucumbers, peppers, loose-leaf lettuce, and herbs.

- Consider hardiness, container size, sunlight exposure, and specific care for growing fruit trees and berries in containers.
- Ensure proper drainage, use quality potting mix, choose suitable container sizes, provide support for climbing plants, and monitor water and nutrient requirements.

IN THE NEXT CHAPTER

Now that you've learned how and when to grow your produce and the ins and outs of taking care of your container garden, you should also know when your crops are ready to be harvested and enjoyed. Next, we will look at when and how to harvest, as well as tips on maintenance and the common mistakes gardeners make that you should avoid.

9

HARVESTING AND MAINTAINING YOUR GARDEN

> *You must give to get; you must sow the seed, before you can reap the harvest.*

— SCOTT REED

GENERAL HARVESTING GUIDELINES FOR CONTAINER GARDENS

Let's delve into the detailed steps and considerations for harvesting produce from your container garden, covering the pre-harvest, during-harvest, and post-harvest stages:

Pre-Harvest

Before harvesting, regularly monitor the maturity of your plants. Different vegetables, herbs, and fruits have specific signs indicating they are ready for harvest, such as color changes, firmness, or size. Refer to plant tags for guidance or research on the specific species.

Harvesting at the right time ensures the best flavor and nutritional content. Avoid harvesting too early or too late, as this can impact taste and quality; for instance, peas have more flavor when picked in the morning, and kale tastes better after the first frost.

Equip yourself with appropriate harvesting tools, such as pruning shears, scissors, or a small knife, depending on the type of crop. Ensure your tools are clean and sharp to minimize damage to plants.

During-Harvest

Handle plants with care to prevent damage to stems, leaves, or fruit. Use a gentle touch, especially when dealing with delicate herbs and soft fruits. Bruising or injuring plants during harvest can affect their post-harvest quality.

Employ suitable techniques for different crops. For leafy greens, use a cut-and-come- again approach, harvesting outer leaves while allowing the inner ones to grow. For fruits, cut or twist them gently from the plant to avoid stress.

Some plants benefit from regular harvesting, promoting continuous production. Harvest herbs frequently—leaving some of the foliage intact—to encourage bushier growth, and pluck ripe fruits promptly to make space for new ones.

Post-Harvest

After harvesting, inspect your plants for any signs of pests or diseases. Freshly pruned plants are more vulnerable to pests. Early detection allows for prompt intervention and prevents the spread of issues to other plants in your container garden.

Clean harvested produce to remove soil, debris, or insects. For certain fruits and vegetables, a gentle rinse is sufficient, while others may require more thorough cleaning.

Store harvested items appropriately. Some crops, like root vegetables, can be stored in a cool, dark place, while others, like leafy greens, benefit from refrigeration. Consider the storage requirements of each crop for optimal longevity and to preserve their quality.

Whenever possible, use freshly harvested produce immediately. This ensures peak flavor and nutritional value. Plan your harvests around mealtime to incorporate the bounty of your container garden into your culinary creations.

MAINTAINING YOUR CONTAINER GARDEN

Tools and Materials

Gather the necessary tools, including a watering can, pruning shears, hand trowel, and gardening gloves. Ensure your containers have proper drainage, and consider using saucers to prevent water damage to surfaces. Quality potting mix and fertilizers specific to container plants are vital for providing essential nutrients.

Water Frequently

Consistent watering is crucial for container plants. Make sure the top two inches or two of the soil is moist, watering only if it's dry. Container gardens may require more frequent watering than traditional gardens, especially during hot weather.

Fertilize Regularly

Container plants rely on the nutrients present in the potting mix, which can deplete over time. Fertilize regularly with a balanced, water-soluble fertilizer during the growing season. Follow the package instructions for proper application to ensure your plants receive adequate nourishment.

Trim and Remove Dead Leaves and Flowers

Keep your container garden tidy by regularly removing dead or yellowing leaves and spent flowers. Pruning your plants will encourage them to put their energy into new growth and prevent potential diseases from spreading. Maintain good air circulation within the containers to reduce the risk of fungal issues.

Change Plants Seasonally

Refresh your container garden by changing plants with each season. Some plants thrive in specific weather conditions, so consider seasonal varieties. This not only adds visual interest but also allows you to explore different plants throughout the year.

Cut Back to Grow More

Prune your plants strategically to encourage bushier growth. Pinch back the tips of herbs and flowers to promote lateral branching. For certain vegetables, like tomatoes,

removing excess foliage redirects energy to fruit production. Regular pruning contributes to healthier and more productive plants.

Prepare for Winter

As winter approaches, prepare your container garden for the colder months. Move plants to a sheltered location if they are not frost-hardy. Mulch the soil surface to insulate roots and protect them from frost. Consider using frost blankets or wraps for added protection. Winter preparation ensures the longevity of your container garden and the well-being of your plants during colder weather.

TIPS FOR A SUCCESSFUL CONTAINER GARDEN

1. Don't Skimp on Drainage

Adequate drainage is essential for preventing waterlogged soil, which can lead to root rot and other issues. Ensure your containers have drainage holes at the bottom to allow excess water to escape. Use a well-draining potting mix to promote a healthy root environment.

2. Evaluate Your Light

Understand the sunlight conditions your garden receives. Different plants have varying light requirements. Choose plants that match the light levels in your space – full sun, partial sun, or shade. Assessing and optimizing light exposure is key to successful container gardening.

3. Feed Your Plants

Plants in containers rely on the provided soil and need regular feeding. Use a balanced, water-soluble fertilizer during the growing season to supply essential nutrients. Follow package instructions for proper application to support robust and healthy plant growth.

4. Make a List Before You Buy Plants

Plan ahead by making a list of plants you want to include in your container garden. Consider the available space, sunlight conditions, and water availability. This list will guide your plant selections, making your shopping experience more focused and efficient.

5. Plant Good Neighbors

Explore companion planting strategies to enhance your garden's overall health. Certain plants complement each other, repelling pests or providing mutual benefits. Understanding the dynamics of companion planting creates a harmonious ecosystem in your container garden. Research and plan your plant arrangements accordingly.

6. Read and Save the Plant Tags

When you purchase plants for your container garden, they often come with tags containing crucial information. These tags provide details on sunlight requirements, watering needs, and potential height and spread of the plant. Save these tags for future reference, as they serve as a handy guide for proper care. Understanding the specific needs of each plant will help you create a suitable environment, ensuring they thrive in your container garden.

7. Acclimate Your Plants

Transitioning plants from the nursery to your container garden requires acclimation. Gradually expose them to outdoor conditions by placing them in their designated spots for increasing periods each day. This process, known as hardening off, helps plants adjust to variations in temperature, sunlight, and wind. Acclimating your plants reduces the risk of transplant shock, promoting healthier and more resilient growth.

8. The More Potting Soil, the Better

Adequate soil volume is crucial for the health of your container garden. Use a generous amount of potting soil to provide ample space for root development. Insufficient soil can lead to overcrowding, restricting root growth and nutrient absorption. Choose a high- quality potting mix, and ensure containers have sufficient depth for robust root systems. Well-nourished roots contribute to stronger, more productive plants.

9. Sometimes Plants Die

Despite your best efforts, some plants may not thrive. Accepting this reality is part of gardening. Various factors, including weather conditions, pests, or disease, can impact plant health. Don't be discouraged by occasional losses. Instead, view them as learning experiences. Assess what might have gone wrong, adjust your care strategies, and consider replacing unsuccessful plants with varieties better suited to your growing conditions.

10. Garden How You Live

Tailor your container garden to align with your lifestyle. Consider the time you can dedicate to maintenance, your aesthetic preferences, and the type of plants you enjoy. Choose low-maintenance plants for a less time-consuming and labor-intensive garden. Choose containers and arrangements that complement your living space, whether it's a balcony, patio, or windowsill. Gardening should be an enjoyable and fulfilling experience, so design your container garden to suit your personal preferences and make it an extension of your lifestyle.

COMMON MISTAKES IN CONTAINER GARDENING

To err is human, especially when trying new things. Be one step ahead by learning from these common mistakes:

Buying Plants That Don't Have the Same Requirements

Each plant has unique needs regarding sunlight, water, and soil conditions. Avoid the mistake of placing plants together in the same container without considering their compatibility. Research the requirements of each plant you intend to include in a container and group those with similar needs. This ensures harmonious growth and prevents competition for resources.

Underfeeding

Container plants rely on the nutrients present in the potting mix, which can deplete over time. Underfeeding your plants by neglecting to fertilize regularly can lead to stunted growth and poor production. A general water-soluble fertilizer is recommended. Apply as per the instructions on the label. Regular application of a balanced fertilizer provides essential nutrients for healthy and vigorous plant development.

Overwatering

It is very easy to overwater container plants and should be done carefully. Always check the moisture level of the soil regularly and before watering so you don't suffocate the roots. Ensure containers have proper drainage so excess water can drain away. Adjust your watering frequency based on environmental factors such as weather and temperature to maintain optimal soil moisture.

Underwatering

On the flip side, underwatering can stress plants and hinder their growth. Container plants, especially those in smaller pots, may require more frequent watering. Monitor the soil moisture consistently and water thoroughly when needed. Adjust your watering schedule based on the specific needs of each plant, considering factors like sunlight exposure and temperature.

Designing an Awkward Plant-to-Pot Ratio

Achieving a balanced and aesthetically pleasing look involves considering the size of your plants in relation to the containers. Planting too many or too few plants in a container can result in an awkward appearance. Before planting, visualize how the plants will fill the container as they grow. Aim for a harmonious balance between the size of the plants and the size of the container to create an appealing and well- proportioned arrangement.

Buying Sick or Weak Plants

Purchasing unhealthy plants sets the stage for disappointment and challenges. Inspect plants for signs of disease, pests, or overall weakness before bringing them home. Choose robust, disease-resistant specimens with healthy foliage. Starting with strong, healthy plants increases the likelihood of a thriving container garden.

Setting Unrealistic Expectations

Unrealistic expectations, such as anticipating rapid growth or abundant harvests in a short time, can lead to frustration. Understand the growth habits and timelines of your chosen plants. Some may take time to establish and produce fruits or flowers. Patience is key in container gardening, and setting realistic expectations ensures a more enjoyable and satisfying gardening experience.

Choosing Containers Made From the Wrong Materials

The material of your containers significantly impacts plant health. Containers made from materials like metal or unglazed terra cotta can absorb and retain heat, potentially harming the roots. Conversely, plastic or glazed containers provide better insulation. Consider the specific needs of your plants and the climate in your area when selecting containers. Opt for materials that promote proper insulation and moisture retention while preventing issues like overheating.

Choosing Containers That Are the Wrong Size

Choosing the right-sized containers is crucial for the health of your plants. Containers that are too small can restrict root growth and lead to waterlogged soil, while overly large containers can hold excess water, risking root rot. Consider the mature size of your plants and choose containers that provide ample space for root development without overwhelming them.

Not Repotting When You Need To

Plants outgrow their containers over time, and neglecting to repot them can hinder their growth. When you notice roots circling the pot or the plant becoming root-bound, it's time to repot. Failing to do so can result in nutrient deficiencies, poor water retention, and stunted growth. Regularly assess your plants and be proactive about repotting to ensure their well-being.

Choosing the Wrong Growing Medium

The type of soil or growing medium directly impacts plant health. Using a generic or poor-quality potting mix can lead to drainage issues, nutrient deficiencies, and compacted soil. Opt for a high-quality potting mix that provides adequate aeration, drainage, and nutrients. Consider adding organic matter to enhance fertility and water retention.

Putting the Containers in the Wrong Place

Container placement is crucial for plant success. Placing containers in areas with insufficient sunlight or excessive wind can adversely affect plant growth. Before arranging your containers, assess the sunlight requirements of your plants and choose appropriate locations. Ensure good air circulation and protection from extreme weather conditions for optimal plant health.

Putting Too Much Effort Into Watering

While consistent watering is essential, overwatering or under-watering can harm plants. Some gardeners, with good inten-tions, may end up stressing plants by either drowning them in water or allowing them to dry out. Understand the water needs of your specific plants and adjust your watering routine accordingly. Consider factors like humidity, temperature, and plant size to strike the right balance.

Not Managing Your Container Garden Organically

Neglecting organic practices in container gardening can lead to the use of chemical fertilizers and pesticides, impacting the environment and potentially harming beneficial organisms. Embrace organic gardening methods such as composting, using natural fertilizers, and implementing companion planting to create a more sustainable and eco- friendly container garden.

Not Giving Container Plants The Support They Need

Container plants, especially those with vining or tall growth habits, may require additional support to prevent bending or breaking. Failing to provide adequate support can lead to structural issues and reduced productivity. Use stakes, cages, or trellises as needed to ensure that plants receive the necessary support for optimal growth and stability.

Not Making the Most of Your Space

Efficient use of space is crucial in container gardening. Overlooking vertical space and neglecting strategic placement can limit the variety and quantity of plants you can grow. Explore vertical gardening techniques, utilize hanging containers, and arrange plants strategically to make the most of your available space, allowing for a diverse and visually appealing container garden.

Not Companion Planting

Extend the concept of companion planting to your containers by choosing plant combinations that promote mutual growth and deter pests.

Not Planting What You Love

Container gardening is a personal endeavor, and the joy of cultivating plants is heightened when you grow what you love. Avoid the mistake of prioritizing practicality over personal preferences. Select plants that bring you joy, whether they are herbs, flowers, or vegetables. Cultivating a container garden filled with your favorite plants enhances the overall gardening experience and encourages a deeper connection with your green space.

IN SUMMARY

- Regularly check plant maturity for optimal harvest, observing color, firmness, and size.
- Handle plants delicately to prevent damage to stems, leaves, or fruit.
- Employ suitable techniques for different crops, such as cut-and-come-again for leafy greens.
- Regular harvesting promotes continuous production for some plants.
- Store items appropriately based on each crop's requirements for optimal longevity.

- Use freshly harvested produce immediately for peak flavor and nutrition.
- Ensure containers have drainage holes to prevent waterlogged soil and root rot.
- Use a balanced, water-soluble fertilizer to provide essential nutrients for robust plant growth.
- Regularly prune leggy growth to encourage bushier, more compact plants for a better overall appearance.
- Understand the growth habits and timelines of plants to set realistic expectations for a satisfying gardening experience.

Enjoying your hard-earned harvest is what gardening is all about. Practicing diligent maintenance ensures that your plants are healthy and comfortable in their containers, contributing to the quality of your gardening experience and harvest. Using the proper tools for pruning, practicing mindful watering and feeding, and regularly assessing your plant's well-being increase your chances of success, reducing the overall amount of maintenance you need to do and freeing up more of your time to enjoy your happy little oasis.

CONCLUSION

In conclusion, this comprehensive guide on container gardening has aimed to empower you to cultivate a thriving and fruitful garden in limited spaces. Absolutely anyone can enjoy the pleasures of growing fresh vegetables, herbs, and fruits, regardless of space constraints.

Key takeaways:

1. Careful selection of vegetable and herb varieties is crucial for successful container gardening.
2. Pay attention to container size, depth, and volume, tailoring them to the specific needs of each plant.
3. Understand the nuances of sunlight exposure and watering, crucial factors in promoting healthy plant growth.
4. Prioritize proper soil drainage, organic matter, nutrient balance, and pH levels for optimal plant development.

5. Use water-soluble fertilizers with a balanced nutrient profile, avoiding over- fertilization.
6. Pay attention to design elements in your garden and plan your space accordingly to make the absolute most of the limited space available.
7. Employ companion planting strategies and crop rotation techniques to enhance plant growth, repel pests, and ensure long-term soil health.
8. Delve into the specifics of growing fruit trees and berries in containers, considering hardiness, container size, and sunlight exposure, as well as plant- specific conditions.
9. Regularly check moisture levels and sunlight exposure to maintain optimal conditions for your plants.
10. Inspect plants often for pests, diseases, and nutrient deficiencies and take prompt action.

With these key principles, you're well-equipped to embark on your container gardening journey. Container gardens generously reward us, returning tenfold when we invest the time and attention they deserve. Opting for a container garden is, in essence, embracing an eco-friendly and sustainable lifestyle choice.

May your path be guided toward making informed decisions for both your personal well- being, that of your plants, and the environment. We trust that this book has ignited a passion within you, empowering you to navigate your gardening journey with passion and confidence!

Your feedback is invaluable, so if you found this guide helpful, please consider leaving a review to help us continue providing valuable insights for the gardening community. Happy gardening, and may your harvests always be plentiful!

REFERENCES

AlfredAustinquotes.(2023a).BrainyQuote.   https://www.brainyquote.com/quotes/alfred_austin_169801

Andrychowicz, A. (2019, April 24). *How to choose the best potting mix for container gardening.* Get Busy Gardening. https://getbusygardening.com/potting-soil-for-container-gardening/

Baessler, L. (2023). *Container garden pest control – dealing with pests in containers.* GardeningKnowHow.   https://www.gardeningknowhow.com/special/containers/container-pests.htm

Baker, N. (2023, February 27). *Our guide to the USDA plant hardiness zones—plus, the best plants to grow in your region.* Martha Stewart. https://www.marthastewart.com/8375670/usda-plant-hardiness-zones

The beautiful benefits of container gardening. (2020, February 18). The Sage. https://blog.gardenuity.com/benefits-container-gardening/amp/

Beck, A. (2021, September 1). *We've broken down the science of composting for you.* Better Homes & Gardens. https://www.bhg.com/gardening/yard/compost/how-to-compost

Benedict, F. (2016, July 7). *5 ways to reduce your carbon footprint with gardening.* Chopra. https://chopra.com/articles/5-ways-to-reduce-your-carbon-footprint-with-gardening

Berry, W., & Wirzba, N. (2010). *The art of the commonplace : The agrarian essays of wendell berry.* Read how you want.

Best container plant combinations.(2023a).Miraclegro. https://miraclegro.com/en-us/projects-planning/best-container-plant-combinations.html

The best watering schedule for houseplants. (2020, August 10). Wild Interiors. https://www.wildinteriors.com/blog/best-watering-schedule-for-houseplants

Brewer, L. J. (2023). *Vegetable and herb gardening in containers.* https://bpb-us-e1.wpmucdn.com/blogs.cornell.edu/dist/c/10116/files/Cornell-Vegetable-and-Herb-Gardening-in-Containers-25g3vpj.pdf

A brief guide to plant hardiness zones for gardens. (2021, December 15). ARK Heirloom Seed Kits. https://heirloomseedkits.com/a-brief-guide-to-plant-hardiness-zones-for-gardens/?gclid=CjwKCAjw4P6oBhBsEiw-

AKYVkqwaN4V1mkveHv0slhdKTBTOmJNHO44ghRP2BdM6IDhC3sp-mOLg5oChoCYosQAvD_BwE

Buiano, M. (2023, February 28). *Vertical gardens are the ideal small-space solution — here are 7 ideas to get started*. Martha Stewart. https://www.marthastewart.com/1535870/vertical-garden-how-to

Choose the best soil for your container garden. (2020, November 9). Brown Thumb Mama. https://brownthumbmama.com/soil-for-container-garden/

Cold composting how to guide.(2017, June 4).Youtube. https://www.youtube.com/watchv=5mfViOHU3_Q&ab_channel=MariaMyGreenGarden

Compost: Feeding your container garden.(2023a). Naples Botanical Garden. https://www.naplesgarden.org/compost-feeding-your-container-garden/

Compost 101 for container gardens. (2021b, September 3).Patio Garden Life. https://patiogardenlife.com/compost-101-for-container-gardens

Conquer small spaces with container gardening - fresh by FTD . (2015, March 13). FTD Blog. https://www.ftd.com/blog/container-gardening

Container gardening. (2016). Celebrate Urban Birds. https://celebrateurbanbirds.org/learn/gardening/container-gardening/

Container gardening: General harvesting guidelines. (2023b). Naples Botanical Garden. https://www.naplesgarden.org/container-gardening-general-harvesting-guidelines

Container gardening basics.(2023). UC Master Gardeners. https://mgsantaclara.ucanr.edu/garden-help/container-gardening/

Container gardening for small spaces. (2022, May 6). Homestead Gardens, Inc. https://homesteadgardens.com/container-gardening-for-small-spaces/

Container gardening for small spaces: Creative garden ideas. (2023, August 31). ECO Gardener. https://ecogardener.com/blogs/news/container-gardening-for-small-spaces

Container gardening made easy: A beginner's guide to growing plants in small spaces . (2023). Swan the Watering Company. https://swanhose.com/blogs/general-gardening/container-gardening-made-easy-a-beginner-s-guide-to-growing-plants-in-small-spaces

Container garden maintenance tips: Help your plants thrive all summer. (2017, June 14). Savvy Gardening. https://savvygardening.com/container-garden-maintenance-tips/

Container gardening 101: Growing food in A small space. (2023, June 14). Chelsea

Green. https://www.chelseagreen.com/2023/how-much-food-can-be-grown-in-a-small-space/

Container gardening with vegetables & herbs tip sheet. (2016, August 25). MSU Extension. https://www.canr.msu.edu/resources/container_gardening_with_vegetables_herbs

Container planting benefits you should know. (2023, May 25). Sonya's Garden. https://sonyasgarden.com/explore-the-garden/top-5-benefits-container-planting

Crowley, T. (2017, August 1). *7 creative vertical gardening techniques that will save you space.*CrowleyLandscapeManagement,Inc. https://crowleyland scape.com/blog/vertical-gardening-techniques/

Decorating small spaces with planters. (2021, January 25). PolyStone Planters. https://www.polystoneplanters.com/planting-tips-1/decorating-small-spaces-with-planters

Earle, C. A. (2021, April 28). *5 ways to compost: Living in small spaces.* EORTH. https://eorth.au/5-ways-to-compost-living-in-small-spaces

Eco-friendly plant pots: Everything you need to know about biodegradable plant pots . (2021, October 5). E-Pots. https://www.e-pots.co.uk/eco-friendly-plant-pots-everything-you-need-to-know-about-biodegradable-pots/

Ecologyaction:FAQ.(2010).EcologyAction. http://www.growbiointensive.org/FAQ/FAQ_CompostingHair.html

18. plants grown in containers | NC state extension publications. (2023). North Carolina State University Extention. https://content.ces.ncsu.edu/exten sion-gardener-handbook/18-plants-grown-in-containers

Environmentally friendly practices for container gardening. (2023). Espace Pour La Vie Montréal.https://espacepourlavie.ca/en/environmentally-friendly-practices-container-gardening

Ersek, K. (2018). *The 6 essential nutrients for healthy plants.* Holganix. https://www.holganix.com/blog/the-6-essential-nutrients-for-healthy-plants

Everything you need to know about container gardening. (2018, August 13). Good Housekeeping. https://www.goodhousekeeping.com/home/gardening/a20707074/container-gardening-tips/

Fertilizing and watering container plants. (2023). Regents of the University of Minnesota. https://extension.umn.edu/managing-soil-and-nutrients/fertilizing-and- watering-container-plants

Flanders, D. (2022, December 22). *How to choose the right container.* HGTV.

https://www.hgtv.com/outdoors/gardens/garden-styles-and-types/how-to-choose-the-right-container

40 garden-fresh vegetable recipes. (2023, April 3). Midwest Living. https://www.midwestliving.com/food/fruits-veggies/vegetable-recipes/

Funes, C. (2021, July 10). *Hot summer tips for water-wise container gardening.* Garden Revelry. https://gardenrevelry.com/summer-waterwise-container-gardening-tips

Gardening in containers.(2023). University of Georgia Extension. https://extension.uga.edu/publications/detail.html?number=C787&title=gardening-in-containers#Soil

Gibson, A. (2010, September 30). *The benefits of container gardening.* The Micro Gardener. https://themicrogardener.com/the-benefits-of-container-gardening/

Gibson, A. (2011, May 28). *15 helpful design tips for vertical gardens.* The Micro Gardener.https://themicrogardener.com/15-helpful-design-tips-for-vertical- gardens/

Gilmer, M. (2023). *The dos and don'ts of handwatering.* Black Gold. https://blackgold.bz/the-dos-and-donts-of-hand-watering/

Gopi. (2019, March 2). *10 essential container gardening tools.* Pinch of Seeds. https://pinchofseeds.com/container-gardening-tools/

Grow berries and fruit in containers / planta. (2023). Get Planta. https://getplanta.com/article/berriesincontainers

A guide to watering plants / RHS campaign for school gardening. (2023). School Gardening. https://schoolgardening.rhs.org.uk/Resources/Info-Sheet/A-Guide-To-Watering-Plants

Hardiness zones in the USA. (2023). Gardenia Creating Gardens. https://www.gardenia.net/guide/united-states-hardiness-zones

Harvest as you grow container gardening. (2023). University of Florida Gardening Solutions. https://gardeningsolutions.ifas.ufl.edu/design/types-of-gardens/havest-as-you-grow-container.html

Hassani, N. (2022, September 17). *20 tips for watering your indoor and outdoor plants.*
The Spruce. https://www.thespruce.com/tips-for-watering-plants-5198467

Haughton, S. (2018, February 13). *Success stories: Owl child care services – John Sweeney garden.* Youth in Food Systems. https://seeds.ca/schoolfoodgardens/success-stories/

Hayes, K. (2012, June 11). *Design ideas for a small space*. Fine Gardening. https://www.finegardening.com/article/design-ideas-for-a-small-space

Hayes, K. (2022, November 21). *The elements of great garden-container design simplified*.FineGardening. https://www.finegardening.com/project-guides/container-gardening/the-elements-of-great-garden-container-design-simplified

Haynes, G. (2023). *Quotes by and about alan chadwick*. Alan-Chadwick. http://www.alan-chadwick.org/html%20pages/quotes.html

Helbig, K. (2021, April 10). *How to compost in small spaces*. Frankie Magazine. https://www.frankie.com.au/article/how-to-compost-in-small-spaces-563158

Herb & vegetable plant combination ideas for container gardens. (2022, April 27). The Sage. https://blog.gardenuity.com/plant-combination-ideas-container-gardens/

Higgins, A. (2018, May 8). Container gardening: The rules to know, and the rules to break.*WashingtonPost*. https://www.washingtonpost.com/lifestyle/home/container-gardening-the-rules-to-know-and-the-rules-to-break/2018/05/07/07c20efe-4a31-11e8-9072-f6d4bc32f223_story.html

Holsinger, A. (2020, June 22). *6 tips for watering container gardens | illinois extension | UIUC*. Extension.illinois.edu. https://extension.illinois.edu/blogs/flowers-fruits-and-frass/2020-06-22-6-tips-watering-container-gardens

How to care for a container garden/miraclegro.(2023b).MiracleGro. https://miraclegro.com/en-us/projects-planning/how-to-care-for-a-container-garden.html

How to design your own container garden - chelsea green publishing. (2023, May 16). Chelsea Green. https://www.chelseagreen.com/2023/how-to-design-your-own-container-garden/

How to make your own compost.(2023, July 7). HouseBeautiful. https://www.housebeautiful.com/uk/garden/a36171927/how-to-make-compost/

How to properly water indoor plants. (2018, November 22). Millcreek Gardens. https://www.millcreekgardens.com/how-to-properly-water-indoor-plants/

Howard, D. G. (2022, April 11). *10 tips for maintaining your container gardens outdoors*. Old Farmer's Almanac. https://www.almanac.com/container-gardening-maintenance

Indoor garden ideas for small spaces: Tips for lush, tiny home gardens. (2023, April

5). Apartment Buds. https://apartmentbuds.com/indoor-garden-ideas-for-small-spaces/

Jackson, V. (2022, November 13). *Drip irrigation pros and cons.* Grow Happier Plants. https://growhappierplants.com/drip-irrigation-pros-and-cons/

Javier, S. (2022, February 14). *4 plant watering methods: Which is best for my plants?* Unbeleafable. https://unbeleafable.ph/plant-watering-methods

Jimerson, D. (2023). *Gardening basics: How to plant a container garden.* Costa Farms. https://costafarms.com/blogs/get-growing/gardening-basics-how-to-plant-a-container-garden

Johnson, K. (2022, April 8). *Helpful tips for creating a successful container garden.* University of Illinois Urbana-Champaign. https://extension.illinois.edu/blogs/good-growing/2022-04-08-helpful-tips-creating-successful-container-garden

Joyner, L. (2022, January 8). *6 ways to lower your garden's carbon footprint in 2022.* House Beautiful. https://www.housebeautiful.com/uk/garden/a38639412/lower-garden-footprint/

Judd, A. (2020, July 4). *Organic pest control that really works.* Growing in the Garden. https://growinginthegarden.com/organic-pest-control-that-really-works/

LaLiberte, K. (2023). *Urban gardening with vegetables in containers | gardener's supply.* Gardeners Supply. https://www.gardeners.com/how-to/urban-gardening-with-vegetables/5491.html

Light, temperature and humidity| ornamental production.(2019).Tamu.edu. https://aggie-horticulture.tamu.edu/ornamental/a-reference-guide-to-plant-care-handling-and-merchandising/light-temperature-and-humidity/

Loughrey, J. (2023). *Container vegetable gardening basics - garden design.* Garden-Design.com. https://www.gardendesign.com/vegetables/container-growing.html

Maintaining container gardens (2023). National Gardening Association. https://garden.org/learn/articles/view/1277/Maintaining-Container-Gardens/

Maintaining container grown vegetables. (2023, February 20). University of Maryland Extension. https://extension.umd.edu/resource/maintaining-container-grown-vegetables

Mangi, T. (2022, September 1). *Organic pest control for a healthy crop.* Global Garden. https://www.globalgarden.co/knowledge/organic-pest-control-for-plants-guide/

Masley, S. (2020). *Choosing containers for container gardening.* Grow It Organically. https://www.grow-it-organically.com/containers-for-container-gardening.html

Maximizing your space: Small indoor gardening ideas. (2023, April 6). Urban Mali. https://www.urbanmali.com/blogs/wisdom/maximizing-your-space-small-indoor-gardening-ideas

May sarton quotes.(2023b).BrainyQuote. https://www.brainyquote.com/quotes/may_sarton_133734

Mays, D., Richter, K., Bradley, L., Sherk, J., Kistler, M., & Neal, J. (2022, February 1).

18. plants grown in containers | NC state extension publications. Content.ces.ncsu.edu. https://content.ces.ncsu.edu/extension-gardener-handbook/18-plants-grown-in-containers

Michael pollan quotes: The single greatest lesson the garden teaches is... (2012, June 27).FamousInspirationalQuotes&Sayings. https://www.inspirationalstories.com/quotes/michael-pollan-the-single-greatest-lesson-the-garden-teaches-is/

Michaels,K.(2019a).*10 container garden tips for beginners.* The Spruce. https://www.thespruce.com/ten-container-garden-tips-for-beginners-847854

Michaels, K. (2019b). *Here's how to grow delicious veggies in containers.* The Spruce. https://www.thespruce.com/vegetable-container-gardening-for-beginners-848161

Michaels, K. (2021, April 13). *10 tips on how to water your container gardens.* The Spruce. https://www.thespruce.com/watering-plants-in-containers-847785

Michaels, K. (2022a, February 14). *10 common container gardening mistakes and how to avoid them.* The Spruce. https://www.thespruce.com/common-container-gardening-mistakes-847796

Michaels, K. (2022b, October 20). *Easy succulent container gardening ideas for beginners.* The Spruce. https://www.thespruce.com/make-a-succulent-plant-container-garden-848006

Morini, R. (2022, November). *Composting options for small, indoor, and restricted spaces.*PiedmontMasterGardeners. https://piedmontmastergardeners.org/article/composting-options-for-small-indoor-and-restricted-spaces/

Must-have gardening tools for container gardens. (2021a, August 22). Patio Garden Life.https://patiogardenlife.com/must-have-gardening-tools-for-container-gardens/

Neveln, V. (2022, June 30). *How to use hardiness zone information to figure out what youcangrow*.BetterHomes&Gardens. https://www.bhg.com/garden ing/gardening-by-region/how-to-use-hardiness-zone-information/

Neveln, V. (2023, August 31). *How to plant a container garden in 6 easy steps.* Better Homes & Gardens. https://www.bhg.com/gardening/container/ basics/how-to-plant-a-container-garden/

Nhất Hạnh, T. (2002). *Anger : Wisdom for cooling the flames.* Riverhead Books.

Noll, M., & Milbrand, L. (2023, June 5). *How to care for succulents—and keep them looking picture-perfect.* Real Simple. https://www.realsimple. com/home-organizing/gardening/indoor/how-to-care-for-succulents

O'Neill, T. (2021, November 20). *Pros vs. cons of drip irrigation in your garden.* Simplify Gardening. https://simplifygardening.com/pros-vs-cons-of-drip-irrigation-in-your-garden/

Organic garden pest control for container gardens. (2014, March 4). Garden365. https://www.garden365.com/container-gardening/organic-garden-pest-control/

Organic pest control for the garden.(2018). Balcony Container Gardening. http:// www.balconycontainergardening.com/wildlife/635-organic-garden-pest-control

Painter, S. (2019, November 18). *Why is soil so important?* Love to Know. https://www.lovetoknow.com/home/garden/why-is-soil-important

Palmer, I. (2021, September 21). *A guide to sustainable container gardening.* House Beautiful. https://www.housebeautiful.com/uk/garden/ a37654320/sustainable-container-gardening/

Patterson, S. (2016, February 4). *15 benefits of container gardening & how to get started.* Natural Living Ideas. https://www.naturallivingideas.com/bene fits-of-container-gardening-how-to-get-started/

Plant nutrients in the soil. (2017). NSW Government Department of Primary Industries. https://www.dpi.nsw.gov.au/agriculture/soils/soil-testing-and-analysis/plant-nutrients

Poindexter, J. (2016, August 17). *13 best fruits and berries you can easily grow in a container garden.* MorningChores. https://morningchores.com/fruits-to-grow-in-containers/

Richmond, J. (2023). *Extension | container gardening.* West Virginia University. https://extension.wvu.edu/lawn-gardening-pests/gardening/creative-gardening/container-gardening

The right soil for container gardening. (2020, March 11). Frugal Family Home.

https://frugalfamilyhome.com/home/gardening/best-soil-for-container-gardening

Robertson, K. (2023, August 8). *8 common garden pests to look for on your plants and how to get rid of them.* BetterHomes&Gardens. https://www.bhg.com/gardening/pests/insects-diseases-weeds/garden-pest-control/

Roll, M., & Wilson, C. R. (2023). *Container Gardens - 7.238.* Colorado State University Extension. https://extension.colostate.edu/topic-areas/yard-garden/container-gardens-7-238

Saeed, M. (2023, March 25). *Composting: A step-by-step guide to creating nutrient-rich soil.* Www.linkedin.com. https://www.linkedin.com/pulse/composting-step-by-step-guide-creating-nutrient-rich-soil-saeed/

Schrader, K. (2020, November 2). *9 space-saving ways to pack more plants into your home.* Apartment Therapy. https://www.apartmenttherapy.com/space-saving-plant-display-ideas-36755826

ScottReedquotes.(2019).BrainyQuote. https://www.brainyquote.com/quotes/scott_reed_121473

The 7 best organic pest control techniques for your garden. (2017, December 18). Good Housekeeping. https://www.goodhousekeeping.com/home/gardening/a20705693/organic-pest-control/

Sharp, J. E. M. (2022, August 8). *The pros and cons of hand watering plants.* Lawn Care Blog | Lawn Love. https://lawnlove.com/blog/pros-and-cons-of-hand-watering-plants/

Shigri, Z. (2023, April 3). *20 creative container garden design ideas for small spaces.* DreamzAR App. https://www.dreamzar.app/post/20-creative-container-garden-design-ideas-for-small-spaces

Singh, J. (2019, January 24). *How to make hot compost complete guide.* Youtube. https://www.youtube.com/watch?v=x4JssQPTYF8&ab_channel=DaisyCreekFarmswithJagSingh

Slim, J. (2019, April 1). *How to plant succulents in container's: A complete guide.* Succulent Plant Care. https://succulentplantcare.com/how-to-plant-succulents-in-containers-a-beginners-guide/

Small space composting - how to compost in a tiny garden. (2021, April 24). ECOgardener. https://ecogardener.com/blogs/news/composting-in-small-spaces

Smith, M. R. (2018, April 4). *Design principles for growing in small space.* Vertical Veg. https://www.verticalveg.org.uk/designing-your-container-garden/

Soil management.(2006).University of Hawai'i. https://www.ctahr.hawaii.edu/ MauiSoil/c_nutrients.aspx

Square vs. round pots for plants: Which is better? (2022, September 29). Flourishing Plants. https://flourishingplants.com/square-vs-round-pots-for-plants/

Stanko, C. (2022, January 5). *30-Minute recipes you can make with ingredients from the garden.* Taste of Home. https://www.tasteofhome.com/collection/ quick-recipes-you-can-make-with-ingredients-from-the-garden/

Stay greener with container gardening. (2021, April 2). The Sage. https://blog. gardenuity.com/stay-greener-with-container-gardening/

Stephens, N. (2023, March 21). *Container garden companion planting guide.* Permaculture Apart. https://www.permacultureapartment.com/post/ container-garden-companion-planting

Sweetser, R. (2022, November 30). *Container gardening with vegetables.* Old Farmer's Almanac. https://www.almanac.com/content/container-garden ing-vegetables

Sweetser, R. (2023, January 13). *10 biodegradable planting pots and how to make your own!* Old Farmer's Almanac. https://www.almanac.com/10-biodegradable-planting-pots-and-how-make-your-own

10 container gardening ideas for small spaces: Balconies and patios. (2023, September 27). Potters Garden Hub. https://pottersgardenhub.com/10-container-gardening-ideas-for-small-spaces-balconies-and-patios/

Tips for the square-inch gardener: Vertical gardening - chelsea green publishing . (2019, July 8). Chelsea Green. https://www.chelseagreen.com/2019/tips-for-the-square-inch-gardener-vertical-gardening-and-the-three-ts

Thetop5apartmentcompostingmethods.(2023).Foodcycler-Production. https:// foodcycler.com/blogs/gardening/the-top-5-small-space-composting-methods

Top5benefitsofcontainerplanting.(2020,July13).Sonya'sGarden. https://sonyasgar den.com/explore-the-garden/top-5-benefits-container-planting/

Vandana, K. (2023, April 20). *How to choose the right containers for your garden.* UrbanMali. https://www.urbanmali.com/blogs/wisdom/how-to-choose-the-right-containers-for-your-garden

Vanover, L. (2020, June 19). *6 tips for watering container gardens.* Birds and Blooms. https://www.birdsandblooms.com/gardening/small-space-gardening/tips-for-watering-container-gardens/

Vartan, S. (2021, July 16). *Cold composting: Step-by-Step guide.* Treehugger.

https://www.treehugger.com/cold-composting-step-by-step-guide-5186100

Vertical gardening ideas, techniques, methods | agri farming. (2018, June 14). Agri Farming. https://www.agrifarming.in/vertical-gardening-ideas-techniques

Vinje, E. (2012, December 7). *How to make compost at home.* Planet Natural. https://www.planetnatural.com/home-composting/

Waddington, E. (2021a, August 13). *12 common container garden mistakes you might be making.* Rural Sprout. https://www.ruralsprout.com/container-garden-mistakes/

Waddington, E. (2021b, December 8). *How to choose containers for a container garden.* Treehugger. https://www.treehugger.com/how-to-choose-containers-garden-5198107

Waddington, E. (2023, June 22). *Expert tips for a sustainable container garden.* Treehugger.https://www.treehugger.com/expert-tips-sustainable-container-garden-7549718

Walliser, J. (2014, May 29). *7 DIY vertical gardening techniques for healthier veggies.* Hobby Farms. https://www.hobbyfarms.com/7-diy-vertical-gardening-techniques- for-healthier-veggies/

Walliser, J. (2017, May 22). *Growing berries in containers: How to grow a small space fruit garden.* Savvy Gardening. https://savvygardening.com/growing-berries-in-containers/

Walliser, J. (2018, March 22). *Container gardening tip list: Advice to help you succeed.* Savvy Gardening. https://savvygardening.com/container-gardening-tip-list/

Ways to reduce your carbon footprint in the garden. (2021, March 22). Borders Organic Gardeners. https://bordersorganicgardeners.org/ways-to-reduce-your-carbon-footprint-in-the-garden/

What do I need for container gardening? (2021, June 3). Gardening Channel. https://www.gardeningchannel.com/container-gardening-supplies-checklist/

What is container gardening? (2017, August 25). Oak Hill Gardens. https://www.oakhillgardens.com/blog/what-is-container-gardening

What is the best soil for container gardening? (+ 5 related faqs) . (2022, July 1). Rosy Soil. https://rosysoil.com/blogs/news/soil-for-container-gardening

Wise, B. (2021, June 1). *Inspiring container gardening stories - how a parent with plants grewaplantparent.*CrescentGarden. https://www.crescentgarden.

com/blog/inspiring-container-gardening-stories-how-a-parent-with-plants-grew-a-plant-parent/

Wohlwend, J. (2020, August 31). *Start A container garden on any porch or patio!* Practically Functional. https://www.practicallyfunctional.com/easy-container-gardening-outdoors/

Woods, S. (2019, January 20). *9 gardening questions to ask yourself if you're A containergardener.*BalconyGardenWeb. https://balconygardenweb.com/gardening-questions-for-container-gardeners/

Made in the USA
Las Vegas, NV
26 February 2024

86361540R00125